Synopsis

Since the mid 1960s, sport has had an explosive growth: many more people now do some form of sport; the Olympic Games are one of the biggest shows on earth, sport is one of the most rapidly increasing industrial sectors. Events to do with sport now hit the front pages (as well as the traditional back ones) of our newspapers. The Heysel tragedy brought home to everyone the bad side of sport; but everyone takes pleasure when one of their heroes wins a gold medal or scores a goal.

The Council of Europe has been promoting participation in sport since 1966 – when it coined the phrase *Sport for All* – and defending the values and contributing to the ethics of sport since 1967 – when it first condemned the doping of athletes. Its work has had a practical effect on all member states, in some of which regular participation is now over 50% of the population. In this book, Jacques Marchand outlines the way in which the Council of Europe has contributed to the biggest phenomenon of modern times, shows how this work is done and gives examples of its impact and relevance to modern man. It is a little known story that deserves a wider audience.

This book will appeal to those interested in sport, to those who work with sport, and equally to students of international relations.

Jacques Marchand, a professional sports journalist on *L'Equipe*, has worked for several years with the Tour de France. He is Honorary President of the French sports journalists' trade union and lives near Paris.

List of Illustrations

(The photographs are from the collection of André van Lierde to whom grateful acknowledgement is made for permission to reproduce them.)

COUNCIL   CONSEIL
OF EUROPE   DE L'EUROPE

01

Sport for All in Europe

95

by
Jacques Marchand

LONDON: HMSO

ISBN 0 11 701489 3

Contents

Foreword

Mr Marchand's book on the Council of Europe and *Sport for All* is not only an excellent summary of our work over the past 20 years – its philosophy, stages, achievements, and effects – but its timely appearance also provides further evidence that sport is one of the major social, cultural and economic phenomena of our times. No government can afford to neglect its promotion and development: it is an essential part of the public provision for a civilised society. Commerce and the mass media are more and more interested and involved in it. More and more Europeans are themselves active members of the sporting world, and share its triumphs and tragedies.

I hope this book will make the Council of Europe's work for *Sport for All* better known. I also hope it will serve as a good example of how the Council of Europe strives to put into practice its concern with individuals to develop their rights and opportunities and thus to improve the quality of life of each and every European, and of Europe as a whole.

Marcelino Oreja
Secretary General
Council of Europe, 1984–9

A matter of growing importance: Sport for all

Dr. Gunther Muller MdB, Chairman of the Committee on Culture and Education of the Parliamentary Assembly of the Council of Europe.

Since January 1970 when the Council of Europe Assembly adopted my first report on the need for a policy on sport for all, a very positive trend has prevailed in the Member States. It has been recognised everywhere that sport is not a privilege to be enjoyed by a few, but a fundamental necessity for everyone. No age group in the population, from small children to senior citizens, is excluded from sport today. Indeed, developments in modern civilisation call for further improvements in sports facilities and activities. As robots begin to take on the heavy physical work in our factories, so it becomes a real need for men and women to exercise their bodies. There is also a need to fill constructively the increasing amount of leisure time at our disposal. In the opinion of one sociologist, the total lifetime's work for each person in our industrial countries will fall to 20,000 hours per capita in the next decades. It is thus imperative to put our leisure time to meaningful use. The diseases of modern civilisation caused by over-eating, drug abuse and lack of physical exercise can be combatted by meaningful sporting activities.

The commercial side of this new trend has long been recognised. The sports and leisure industry is the fastest growing sector in Europe. Whereas a ball used to be the most important item of sports equipment, people now spend millions on surf-boards or hang-gliders. In spite of this tendency, the most prevalent interest is still spectator sport: watching others play from a seat in the stadium or from a T.V. armchair. This fact has again been demonstrated by the television programme ratings for the world football matches. For this reason alone, it is necessary to do more for the promotion of sport by public authorities and, above all, to support private initiatives in clubs. We call upon local and national authorities to make available the necessary playing facilities and sports fields, gymnasia and swimming baths. This will help to give the general public all the facilities which are necessary in order to participate in sport on a really large scale.

However, sport for all still needs stars and ideals. For example, we have seen in the Federal Republic of Germany how the winner of Wimbledon in 1985 and 1986 has popularised tennis in that country. Many events – and I am thinking here in particular of the mass running contests and walks – put the capacity of the participants to a real test.

Sports and games are an excellent preparation for politics. There are rules to be observed just as there is competition and success or failure. Politicians are also expected to abide by the 'rules of the game'. In our mass society, no longer characterised by a common circle of friends and neighbours in an idyllic village setting, educating people to practise fair play represents one of the basic conditions for maintaining a democratic consensus. To this extent, the old Roman proverb about keeping a healthy mind in a healthy body – *mens sana in corpore sano* – has now acquired a completely new dimension.

Sport for All:
Comprehensive in range,
humanistic in aim

One day in 1968 (17 January):

● Kirt George Kiesinger, Chancellor of the Federal Republic of
Germany, announcing a forthcoming visit to Paris said 'We must
take General de Gaulle at his word, when he says that the
European Economic Community is political, as well as economic
. . .'

● Urho Kekkonen, President of Finland, following elections to the
300-strong electoral college, was assured of a third six-year term
of office.

● Mr Jenkins, British Chancellor of the Exchequer, announced an
austerity budget, with increases in direct and indirect taxation.
Harold Wilson confirmed that British troops were to be with-
drawn from Singapore and Malaysia, a prospect which gave rise
to great anxiety in Asia.

● The Austrian skiers, Olga Pall and Christl Has, came first and
second in the World Cup downhill race in Badgastein.

The same day (17 January 1968):

At the Ter Groene Poorte (Green Gateway) leisure centre, in Bruges,
Armand Lams, administrative director of Belgium's National Institute of Physical Education and Sport, in his capacity as Chairman of
the Sport Section of the Council of Europe's Committee for Out-of-
School Education, hosted a meeting attended by William Jones,
Secretary-General of ICSPE and the International Amateur Basketball Federation; Cecrope Barilli, Italian national delegate; Yvonne

1

Surrel, French Inspector General of Youth and Sport; and Gerard Herberichs, a Dutchman, Principal Administrative Officer in charge of the Council of Europe Sport Section. These five were the members of the Planning Group.

In welcoming them, the chairman said that the meeting would have to go on for three days, virtually non-stop, in order to deal with the three items on the agenda, ie:

1. to define what could be included in the idea of *Sport for All*, which had been in the air for several years

2. to assess what this activity would require and outline a long-term programme

3. to choose the projects to be started in 1968 and 1969.

The small group got straight down to work, starting with a study of several experts' reports on their countries' experiments in new kinds of physical activity within everyone's capabilities. The reports were by Birch (UK), Caginal (Spain), Eklow (Sweden), Palm (Federal Republic of Germany) and Vlot (Netherlands). The group also looked at the study of physiological and social aspects of physical fitness carried out at the request of the Secretary General of the Council of Europe by Per-Olof Åstrand of Sweden.

Why did this meeting of the Planning Group of the Sport Section of the Committee for Out-of-School Education attract more attention from Council of Europe experts than other meetings of a similar nature, to such an extent that they regarded it as being historic? Although every working meeting over the years laid its own stone in the edifice of the charter and contributed to the creation of a European sports policy the Bruges meeting, more than any of the others, came at a turning point and transformed a number of ideas – which had been circulating among top sports officials and expressed in different languages – into clear, well-argued principles.

These principles and the arguments put forward in their support consolidated and gave official status to the still tentative experiments in physical activity for all, while at the same time outlining a common European policy. In 1975, after a seven-year period of gestation and reflection, they gave birth to the European *Sport for All* Charter.

The term *Sport for All* itself was not new, having appeared in Council of Europe documents as early as 1966. Jurgen Palm, head of Germany's Sport for All office (regarded as one of the original pioneers of the movement), has confirmed that certain countries, including the Nordic nations, had adopted it as early as 1960. However, the Bruges meeting can claim the credit for producing a precise definition of the concept of sports activities open to every section of the population, though this definition may subsequently have been forgotten or distorted in some countries.

2

The meeting report notes that 'sport . . . is to be understood in the modern sense of free, spontaneous physical activity engaged in during leisure time; its functions . . . being recreation, amusement and relaxation. Sport in this sense includes sports proper and various other physical activities provided that they demand some effort'. 'All' is defined as the widest possible range of the population, of both sexes and of all ages. The group did not wish to lay down a permanent text but adopted the following conclusion: *Sport for All* must provide 'conditions to enable the widest possible range of the population to practise regularly either sport proper or various physical activities calling for an effort adapted to individual capacities'.

Has *Sport for All* in fact remained faithful to its original, historical definition? That is open to discussion – the Council of Europe makes suggestions, but leaves it to each member state to decide how it will apply the common policy. This idea of flexibility for each nation means that each can adapt the definition to suit itself. Some have found apt wording: Finland has changed *Sport for All* into 'sport as a means of keeping fit', defined as 'a physically active lifestyle'. And in its 'Idrottat Ålla' (Sport for All) report, Sweden reveals a concept not far removed from Finland's: all physical activities, whether competitive or not, which people undertake in order to achieve a specific result or for the sake of exercise and physically active recreation are to be considered as sport.

The mistake that a great many government officials, sports administrators and journalists now make is to lump together *Sport for All*, 'mass sport' and 'popular sport' in sharp contrast to top-class sport. In France, where the federations have not always been able to understand or accept the fact that spontaneous sport is becoming widespread, the *Sport for All* concept is often presented as an antidote to too much spectator sport, and it is seen to clash, in spirit and philosophy, with 'top level sport'. The latter certainly receives more support, and its very name implies that sport exists at another (avoiding the term 'lower') level. The distinction between the two is sufficiently deep-rooted in the minds of French sports officials for Jacques Chaban-Delmas[1] to have told them, at the opening of the 3rd international *Sport for All* colloquy, in Bordeaux (November 1986) that 'It is a sin of the mind to contrast top-class sport with sport for the masses'.

The French are surely not the only sinners in this respect. In the Federal Republic of Germany, where sport is better regulated than in its neighbour across the Rhine, a clear distinction is made between 'Leistungssport' (high performance sport), the 'Zwweiter Weg' (second path) and 'Trimm Dich Durch Sport' (keep fit through sport). This last is the German contribution to the international 'Trim' movement, which originated in Norway and is intended to make people aware of the need to take physical exercise.

The three-day meeting in Bruges not only defined *Sport for All* back in 1968 and pointed it in the chosen direction, but it also justified its own action on the basis of three essential arguments:

1. Biological and Medical

Statistics show that lack of physical exercise in industrial societies is a greater source of ill-health than infections or cancer[2], so health and social security budgets can make substantial savings if people take up sport. It ought therefore to be possible to convince the authorities and the private sector of both the biological and medical needs and the good financial sense of encouraging people to engage in sport.

2. Social

For a long time, sport was a luxury. This was already so when the games of antiquity took place, and it remained so at the time of Baron Pierre de Coubertin. Indeed, while the specific values of sport are undisputed, and have even been recognised for tens of centuries, only a minority of the privileged have enjoyed the physical and moral benefits of sport's contribution to personal development. So conditions will have to be created which will enable everyone to participate in sports activities, particularly the most underprivileged groups: women, children, old people, migrants, the disabled, prisoners and other offenders.

This does not prevent – indeed, it encourages – the inclusion of measures which contribute to the development and protection of high performance sport (such as those against doping and violence in sports grounds). The Council of Europe will also study developments that may cause the authorities problems in respect of financial support for sport, and new types of co-operation with sponsors and the media.

3. Human

Man is a social creature, unable to live alone. He has a vital need to communicate. The warmth of genuine human relations is essential to his security and balance. Yet what does he find in today's industrial society?

He experiences the constraints of employment, with its enforced rhythms and its extreme, mechanised specialisation. He feels the anguish of losing his job, being unemployed and having nothing to do. Life is often confined within large housing units, supermarkets, self-service cafeterias and the hassle of public transport. He runs the risk of a nervous breakdown unless he can compensate for these pressures and restore his balance through frequent contact with nature, expending physical energy and emulating others. Play, an integral part of culture, provides opportunities for satisfying the need for self-expression and creation felt by men and women of all ages, whatever their class and nationality.

By putting forward these three facts, the Planning Group was quite simply asserting the humanistic nature of sport which is open to all. If we are to understand the slow but sure intellectual process that culminated in this concept of sport, embracing human and social elements, we must look closely at the context in which the concept evolved: that of the Council of Europe itself. What is the Council of Europe? In order to answer that and to better grasp its interest in sport, we shall have to find out why the Council exists and what it does.

Notes:

(1) Mayor of Bordeaux and President of the French National Assembly, but also a former tennis and rugby international.

(2) Infectious diseases have been efficiently controlled, but degenerative diseases, especially cardio-vascular disorders have become more widespread, accounting for more than half of all natural deaths in some countries (as reported by Professor Per-Olof Åstrand, of Sweden).

The Council of Europe: History, machinery and organisation

From the balcony of the Hotel de Ville, Winston Churchill greeted the crowds with his V-sign. It was 11 August 1949, and the British bulldog whose courage and tenacity had halted the surge of Nazism across Europe was acclaimed by the people of Strasbourg as both a hero and a symbol.

That same day, he attended the first sitting of the Assembly of the Council of Europe, which chose as its first president Paul-Henri Spaak of Belgium, and made the Speaker of the French National Assembly, Edouard Herriot, an honorary president in acknowledgement of his efforts to promote international co-operation.

But it was Winston Churchill who inspired the people of Alsace: they saw in him the spiritual father of the Council of Europe. He claimed no title, content just to give it his backing. As far back as 1943, in a speech on the radio at the height of the storm in which he had promised his fellow-countrymen blood and tears, he foresaw the need to build a united Europe after the war. This would be a logical development and a sensible move towards an international diplomatic network resulting in stronger, more deeply-rooted democracies.

The Congress of Europe in the Hague in May 1948 brought together official delegates from sixteen European nations and observers, including exiles, from nine. They agreed to call for a European Assembly, a European Charter and a Court of Human Rights. Winston Churchill's idea was gaining ground. A small-scale Europe of five nations (Belgium, France, the Netherlands, Luxembourg and the United Kingdom) already existed. The Brussels Treaty Organisation tried in the same year (1948) to lay down rules for military, economic, social and cultural co-operation among neighbours: a simple starting point for a wider, more ambitious European community making it possible 'to associate progressively in the pursuance of (its) aims other states inspired by the same ideals and animated by the like determination'[1].

In March 1949, Denmark, Ireland, Italy, Norway and Sweden boarded the European train as it pulled out of the station. The five-nation Europe doubled in size, and ministers of the ten nations met at St. James' Palace, in London, on 5 May, to sign the Council of Europe's birth certificate. It was not by chance that London was chosen as the location for this historic act: the choice was made in recognition of the efforts of Winston Churchill and his nation. Nor was Strasbourg selected at random as the home of the Council of Europe. The Rhine, which divides nations of Europe once at war with each other, is now a symbol of the desire for reconciliation.

It was not long before the original ten nations of the 1949 group became twelve, with the addition of Greece and Turkey (in August 1950), and then fourteen, including Iceland and the Federal Republic of Germany, the last-named being admitted as an associate member in July 1950 and as a full member in May 1951. Today, with its twenty-three nations[2], the Council of Europe represents 400 million people in an area extending from Iceland in the north-west to Turkey in the south-east.

However, this historical description would be incomplete unless emphasis were laid on the main idea, or ideas, that led statesmen to reconcile their countries with each other and unite them. We must never lose sight of the fact that when the Council of Europe excluded from its scope military and defence questions – for which NATO is responsible – it set itself the main objectives of improving the living conditions of citizens of member states, developing human values, defending the principles of parliamentary democracy and defending human rights.

Once the institution had been recognised and found a home in Strasbourg, how did it subsequently organise, structure and finance itself, so as to fulfil its aims and carry out its chosen programme? Two statutory organs set the system in motion: the Committee of Ministers, which provides a direct link with governments, and the Parliamentary Assembly, representing the national parliaments which provide its members. The two have different roles.

The *Committee of Ministers* is in fact a committee of the foreign ministers of the 23 member states: they each represent their government when major decisions are taken by the organisation and when the direction of future efforts is laid down. As a political committee and decision-making body, the Committee has three rules for voting: political decisions and major recommendations require unanimity, while a two-thirds majority is needed for budget decisions and a majority is sufficient for procedural decisions. Between sessions, their work is prepared by meetings of the Ministers' Deputies (the permanent representatives of their governments).

In the fields of co-operation covered by the Council of Europe, including both culture and sport, there is frequent recourse to technical committees of experts comprising government officials and, sometimes, representatives of non-governmental organisations (NGOs). The CDDS (Steering Committee for the Development of Sport) is one of the few such mixed committees. As the Ministers for Foreign Affairs considered that the Council of Europe's objective of greater unity could be facilitated by direct contacts between the members of governments responsible for specific areas of government activity, so they have over the last twenty years adopted the practice of seeking the assistance of colleagues more *au fait* with matters concerning them directly. Health and social security questions are considered by a conference of member states' health ministers, while matters relating to education, culture and justice are similarly discussed by conferences of member states' appropriate ministers. Sport, too, has had its own conference of ministers since 1975.

The *Parliamentary Assembly* is a forum and a place for free expression of European opinion; could it not ultimately be the conscience of democratic Europe?

When it was first set up, under the name 'Consultative Assembly', it was the first ever international parliamentary assembly. It still has only consultative power, but the conclusions of its debates reach governments via the Committee of Ministers, in the form of recommendations. The Assembly meets for about three weeks per year in the central chamber of the Palais de l'Europe. The chamber seats 500 and has a copper roof, supported by great mahogany arches. In addition to the two official languages of the Council of Europe (English and French), there are facilities for simultaneous interpretation into a further seven languages, and German, Italian and Spanish are commonly used.

The Assembly's work, like that of the Committee of Ministers, is largely done by committees in the interval between sessions. These committees submit their conclusions to the Assembly, so that the latter can hear what the rapporteur has to say and then debate and vote on the subject. Votes are taken either on recommendations to the Committee of Ministers (in which case a two-thirds majority is required for adoption) or on draft resolutions (requiring just a majority), which are sent directly to recipients – the governments or institutions concerned with the subject – by the President of the Assembly. However, information about the Council or Europe's work in the sphere of sport may also be sent directly to international sports federations or the IOC.

The Assembly has found a potential method of evading the authority of the Committee of Ministers, the only organ with decision-making powers: it has set up a committee on parliamentary and public relations, enabling it to make its views on certain subjects known directly and to bring pressure to bear to get a trend accepted

8

or to promote a scheme if necessary.

The members of the Council of Europe's Parliamentary Assembly are not elected by universal suffrage, as are their 518 colleagues and neighbours of the European Community's parliament, which also meets under the copper roof of the Palais de l'Europe. The 177 members of the Council of Europe's Assembly are appointed by the parliaments of their own nations, each country having a number of representatives proportionate to the size of its population. While France, the Federal Republic of Germany, Italy and the United Kingdom have 18 seats each, Spain and Turkey have only twleve, and Liechtenstein makes do with two.

The membership of national delegations reflects the balance of power between the political parties in each country. Therefore, Strasbourg inevitably sees a reconstitution of the major international political families: socialists, christian democrats, conservatives, liberals and communists.

Since its foundation, the Council of Europe has chosen between different nationalities and political allegiances when electing Presidents of the Assembly: Paul-Henri Spaak (Belgium), a socialist (1949–51); Francois de Menthon (France), of the MRP (1952–54); Guy Mollet (France), a socialist (1954–56); Fernand Dehouses (Belgium), a socialist (1956–59), John Edwards (United Kingdom), of the Labour Party (1959); Per Federspiel (Denmark), a liberal (1960–63); Pierre Pflimlin (France), of the MRP (1963–66); Sir Geoffrey de Freitas (United Kingdom), of the Labour Party (1966–69); Olivier Reverdin (Switzerland), a liberal (1969–72); Giuseppe Vedovato (Italy), a Christian Democrat (1972–75); Karl Czernetz (Austria), a socialist (1975–78); Hans J de Koster (Netherlands), a liberal (1978–81); Jose Marie de Areilza (Spain), a liberal (1981–83); Karl Ahrens (Federal Republic of Germany), a socialist (1983–86); Louis Jung (France), a Christian Democrat (1986–89) and Anders Björck (Sweden), a European Democrat (1989–).

The Assembly elects judges to the European Court of Human Rights, which shares a nearby building on Place du President Robert Schuman with the European Commission of Human Rights. It also elects the Secretary General, who is responsible to the Committee of Ministers for the Council of Europe's administrative machinery, involving 850 officials from various nations, but who work in French and English.

The Palais de l'Europe was inaugurated by the President of the French Republic, Valery Giscard d'Estaing, on 28 January 1977. The French architect Henry Bernard designed the building and supervised work on it for five years. He explained that he had tried, through the external geometry of the building, to express strength in unity. In the interior design he tried to create a serene and happy atmosphere, friendly, self-assured and conducive to the free exchange of conflicting ideas.

9

The reception area, dominated by soaring mahogany arches, resembles a station concourse: it is a bustling place. This is not surprising, as the Council of Europe plays host to a lot of people. These include ministers, who have their own, round room; members of the Assembly, who have their chamber; officials and other staff, who have 700 offices at their disposal and journalists, who have the use of a press room and radio and television studios. Representatives of Europe's municipalities and regions and a European Youth Centre with more than a thousand young people of every nationality add to the noise and the atmosphere.

The Palais de l'Europe, which cost 215 million francs to build in 1977, has space to receive these people, with its 64,000m^2 of floorspace on 9 levels; 40,000m^3 (100,000 tonnes) of concrete went into the building. Shining on the activities of an organisation which has nothing to hide, the light pours in through 8,000m^2 of windows.

Now that we have looked at the Council of Europe as a whole – its birth and development, its structure and premises and the machinery enabling it to operate, it is time to get back to the particular, by scrutinising the sector which is of special interest to us: sport and physical activities. It will be easier to appreciate the sequence and inter-relationship of events if we first look at the history of this sector. If we go back to the beginning, we can trace all the Council of Europe's efforts in the sphere of sport. These may have been slow, but they were sure.

Sport was at first entrusted to the cultural sector, which passed it on to education. To be precise, it came under 'out-of-school education'. The next step took the Council of Europe towards the setting up of the CDDS (Committee for the Development of Sport) and, more importantly, towards the drafting of the European *Sport for All* Charter.

Notes:

(1) Leon Marchal, when Secretary General of the Council of Europe.

(2) The 23 member states are, in alphabetical order, Austria, Belgium, Cyprus, Denmark, Finland, France, Federal Republic of Germany, Greece, Iceland, Ireland, Italy, Liechtenstein, Luxembourg, Malta, Netherlands, Norway, Portugal, San Marino, Spain, Sweden, Switzerland, Turkey and the United Kingdom. Two other states, the Holy See and Yugoslavia participate fully in inter-governmental co-operation in the spheres of culture, education and sport, which are governed by the European Cultural Convention.

3

The European Charter and the birth of the CDDS

The European Cultural Convention, drawn up in 1954 for member states – but to which the Holy See and Yugoslavia have also acceded – encompasses sport and physical activities, which it suggests should be used as a means of education.

In 1960, the education and culture elements of the Brussels Treaty were transferred to the Council of Europe. Thus the committee of cultural experts – which in 1962 became the Council for Cultural Co-operation (CCC) – took over responsibility for physical education and sport. The very first national surveys revealed that a large number of Europeans engaged in physical activities or sport, so the CCC asked the Committee for Out-of-School Education to study the situation more closely and submit proposals to it.

From that point onwards, the structure began to take shape, formed by ideas and schemes which were in turn shaped by a number of studies.

The Committee for Out-of-School Education was impressed by a study by J Dumazedier and A Ripert, who write in *Loisir et Culture* that 'the people of 1985, confined in increasingly crowded towns and constrained to even more highly organised activities, will feel a physical need for exercise'.

At about the same time, towards the end of 1969, Gunther Muller, the German rapporteur to the Consultative Assembly, suggested that the Assembly launch a *Sport for All* campaign based on the achievements in some member states, including the Federal Republic of Germany, Norway, the Netherlands, Sweden and Spain. He asked for national structures to be set up for the movement in each country and for an international co-ordinating body to be created at the Council of Europe.

The report also served as a reminder that *Sport for All* was on the

11

move throughout the world. Examples came from the countries of eastern Europe – the USSR, Poland and Czechoslovakia, which were not the last to prepare policies for popular sport – also from the USA where President Kennedy had launched the 'National Fitness' campaign, and from Australia, with its already existing National Fitness Council.

The next step was the European colloquy in Strasbourg, opened on 14 September 1970 by William Jones, a prominent figure of British birth. He kept up his reputation of seeming more Germanic than British by wearing his traditional bow tie, smoking large cigars and quaffing good beer – generally in Munich, where he was a leader of the International Amateur Basketball Federation.

He was invited to chair the colloquy on European sport, which was attended by such eminent figures that it was surely the most important meeting held on the subject, because he had been a member of the Bruges group in 1968 and was involved from the outset in the debate. The Assembly intended to consider what had been said before outlining decisions for proposal to the CCC. For three days, papers were presented and lectures delivered in Strasbourg, and they remain reference documents to this day[1].

Gunther Muller presented another report to the Assembly's committee on culture in 1971, in which he said that 'in the 14 months since the Assembly debate on Recommendation 588, there have been important new developments which show that *Sport for All* is at present undergoing a phase of rapid and decisive progress, both within member states and at European level'.

That same year, the CCC recommended that the Committee of Ministers bring the Clearing House, an information centre which the Belgian Government intended to set up to cover the planning and activities of *Sport for All*, under the aegis of the Council of Europe. Mr Muller had also urged the Consultative Assembly to recognise this information centre, which was intended to be the focal point of exchanges of information and experiences relating to the various sports activities tried out by member states.

Also at about the same time, Gerard Herberichs was able to tell the Panathlon International Congress in Venice that: '*Sport for All* is both a concept and a political fact . . . The originality of the concept is due to the fact that it considers sport essentially from the viewpoint of its social or potential social functions. The difference between this concept and the traditional concept of sport, a mere game which only involved individuals, (is that its) function in yesterday's society was to divert the happy few, a minority of enthusiasts or of socially privileged people.' Today, 'recreational sport is becoming an essential part . . . of everyday life of the citizens in all industrialised countries.'

Increasingly convinced by Gunther Muller, its rapporteur, that sport for all was part and parcel of European social and cultural policy, on 14 May 1971 the Consultative Assembly decided to study a draft European Charter. For the next few years, efforts were concentrated on the drafting of this Charter.

The indefatigable Muller said in the 1972 explanatory memorandum to the preliminary draft that *Sport for All* encompassed established sports, open-air activities, aesthetic activities and keep-fit programmes. A skilled expert was asked to do the drafting; this was Alistair D Munrow, Director of Physical Education at the University of Birmingham, UK. When Gerard Herberichs wrote to him in February 1972, setting out a precise timetable of meetings in Strasbourg, Vienna and Paris, he explained that the Charter was intended to become the basis of a complete system of co-operation and would have to formulate and codify the new principles.

The Secretariat was instructed to collect suggestions for the Charter from sports organisations, and the Committee for Out-of-School Education, for its part, set up a co-ordinating group comprising 3 government representatives, 3 members of NGOs (non-government organisations) and an independent expert.

In 1974 the Committee of Ministers approved the CCC's proposal to make sport a separate sector and to set up an ad hoc consultative meeting bringing together representatives of sports organisations, both governmental and non-governmental.

On 28 June 1974, an initial revised version of the Charter (dated 1 June 1974), presented by Mr Harold Sagar (United Kingdom), was submitted to the ad hoc meeting and its working party, which included among its members Max Wasterlain, Belgium's Director-General of Physical Education, Sport and Outdoor Activities, K Moeller, Chairman of the Dansk Idraets-Forbund, N G Vlot, of the Sports Federation of the Netherlands, Nelson Paillou, of the French National Olympic and Sports Committee and W Winterbottom, director of the British Sports Council.

December saw discussion in Strasbourg of the third version of the Charter and comments thereon, while the fourth was adopted by the ad hoc meeting in January 1975 for proposal to the European Ministers for Sport. The Clearing House had also played a very active part in its preparation, collecting and summarising information about experiments which were in progress.

At the same time as this text was being slowly and meticulously drafted, the Committee of Ministers (Ministers of Foreign Affairs) was entrusting to conferences of specialised ministers the responsibility for studying matters within their spheres. Thus 'Sport' was to be discussed by a Conference of Ministers Responsible for Sport, and to give its opinion on the Charter which had been prepared for it.

It did so in Brussels on 20 March 1975, an historic date, since it was the day on which the Charter was promulgated prior to its endorsement and official adoption on 24 September 1976 by the Committee of Ministers, the highest organ of the Council of Europe.

13

This historic date was also that of the first meeting of the world's Ministers Responsible for Sport and Physical Activities, something that would have been unthinkable only a few years ago, as noted by Mr B Gjerde, Norway's Minister of Education and Culture[2].

At 9.30am on Thursday, 20 March 1975, at the Palais d'Egmont, Mrs R de Backer-Van Ocken, Belgium's Minister for Dutch Culture, welcomed her European colleagues and invited Mr S Sforza, Deputy Secretary General of the Council of Europe, to inaugurate the conference. It was to prove rich in ideas, some of which we shall analyse later in various stages of this study.

The Charter meant that European sport had a programme from 1975 onwards, but it was up to the Council of Europe to carry it out and make sure that member states implemented it. The first thing it had to do was acquire the necessary resources.

Mr D Howell, the United Kingdom Minister of State, said at the Brussels conference, '... it is now totally inappropriate to leave (sport) within the remit of the Out-of-School Education Committee of the Council for Cultural Co-operation'. The conference adopted a resolution calling for the ad hoc consultative meeting to be trans-formed into the Council for the Development of Sport (CDS). The recommendation was accepted virtually as it stood: the ad hoc meeting which had fathered the Charter was initially maintained and then became a sport committee of the CCC.

At long last sport became self-sufficient through the setting up of the Committee for the Development of Sport (CDDS), in 1977. This is an independent body directly answerable to the Committee of Ministers, to which its submits proposals based on the recommenda-tions put forward by the Conference of European Ministers for Sport.

The CDDS is the link between the Committee of Ministers and the conference of sport ministers, and it retains its connection with the Council for Cultural Co-operation, which is still concerned with certain matters, such as sport in schools. Up to four representatives of each member state may sit on the Committee, which comprises experts, senior officials of both government and non-government bodies and individuals with responsibility for their countries' sports policies. Hence the CDDS, the driving force behind European sports policy, is the dynamo which converts the principles of the Charter into facts and activities.

Notes:

(1) *Physiological and social aspects of physical fitness* (Per-Olof Åstrand)
   Some thoughts on the place of sport in social cultural policy (Alistair C Munrow)
   Trimm Dich Durch Sport (keep fit through sport), a campaign conducted in the

Federal Republic of Germany (Jurgen Palm)
Sport for All in Spain (Manuel Giner Gallardo)

(2) The UNESCO conference in 1976 and the 1978 Charter constituted a global extension of the work of the Conference of Ministers.

4

The desire for, and development of, European co-operation

'The willing co-operation of friendly nations to work together to develop sport policies has implications for Europe beyond purely those of sport', according to a CDDS report submitted to the third Conference of European Ministers for Sport. This was six years after the Charter was issued and shows that the effects of the Charter were beginning to make themselves felt.

It had taken time, as was to be expected. It had first been necessary to instil the political will expressed in Article 1 of the Charter:

'Every individual shall have the right to participate in sport'.

The first version had gone further:

'. . . and shall not be prevented by lack of opportunity'.

When the ad hoc meeting examined the original text of the Charter it amended the wording more than the general idea. By suggesting that the second part of the sentence be deleted in order to increase the impact of the part that remained, the working party made the fundamental principle ring out like a watchword. That is what it is. If it is regarded as each citizen's right to engage in sport – a right that is enshrined in some countries' constitutions and laid down by law in others, such as the Grand Duchy of Luxembourg – the State has to guarantee that it is possible for them to do so.

'Real opportunities to participate are a pre-requisite of the right to participate. It must therefore be a major task for us to see it to that such opportunities become a reality for all', according to the Norwegian Minister, Mr B Gjerde, at the Brussels conference in 1975.

Article 1 says it all in eight words. It makes calls upon both individual and collective responsibility, summoning:

- *citizens to engage in sport,*

- *governments to adopt or adapt provisions enabling them to do so,*

- *and the Council of Europe itself to maintain an atmosphere of political co-operation between member states in order to encourage them to do so.*

Co-operation is obviously essential, but upon what should it be based? Pierre Mazeaud, French State Secretary for Youth and Sport, tried to identify this basis when he addressed the Brussels conference, saying that as in all other sectors, European co-operation on sport must be striven for. Sport, a 'social phenomenon', was an essentially political area for co-operation.

At the same conference Mr H F Van Aal (Belgium's Minister for French Culture) expressed his view that although charters were not documents and had no binding force, they nevertheless had considerable moral weight and could provide a sound basis for a genuinely European policy.

But Pierre Mazeaud had also said at the conference that sport was still 'mainly private', and that state intervention was therefore desirable in the form of grants, but not in other forms. He even spoke of a hiatus in relations between states and international sport, exemplified by the case of the Olympic Games. He said that the states which hosted the Games were directly involved and played a major role in organising them, but that they had no part in the IOC's decision-making process.

This French mountaineer-turned-minister was already presaging the differences of opinion as to whether or not athletes ought to participate in the Moscow Games, which later divided certain governments – such as the French and British – from their countries' sports bodies. But his unambiguous viewpoint was not fully shared by all his colleagues. Aware that the state's role in sport policy varied from country to country, with some governments taking control and others adopting a liberal attitude, the CDDS has always tried to strike a balance and ensure that government and non-government bodies have complementary roles.

Mr S Sforza, Deputy Secretary General of the Council of Europe, in his speech inaugurating the Brussels conference, said that he attached the greatest importance to the planned establishment of co-operation machinery within the Council of Europe. Such machinery would accurately reflect the way in which sport was organised in member states, be capable of determining how sport should progress along the path laid down in the Charter and provide the surest way of moving towards the set objectives. The rate of joint achievements and the intensification of co-operation would depend on the efficiency of the machinery.

Since the Brussels conference, the intensity of co-operation in various fields has been illustrated by a series of formal conferences of European Ministers for Sport: in London (1978), Palma de Majorca (1981), Malta (1984), Dublin (1986) and Reykjavik (1989), interspersed by informal meetings: in London (1975), Bonn (1976), Strasbourg (1977, 1980 and 1985), Lisbon (1977 and 1985), Paris (1977, 1978 and 1983), Athens (1979 and 1989) and Rotterdam (1983), at which current problems had been urgently dealt with. Thanks to studies that had already been carried out, it was possible for example to draw up the European Convention on spectator violence and misbehaviour at sports events less than two months after the Heysel tragedy. Another example of European co-operation is the work on the CDDS in preparing documents for the ministerial conferences and in co-ordinating and boosting schemes in member states.

Co-operation has achieved a great deal over the past ten years, but statistics cannot fully reflect the influence of resolutions and the Charter. However, we do have reference points arising from the formal Conferences of Ministers for Sport that take place at three year intervals.

The 1978 conference in London was still concerned with implementation of the Charter, chaired by the British Minister, Chris Howell. It brought together the national reports and made a first assessment of progress, concluding that the Charter had had beneficial effects on *Sport for All*. The same conference brought confirmation of the role of the CDDS, which had been given greater powers through its elevation by the Committee of Ministers to steering committee status in November 1977. Another crucial decision was that the CDDS was to be responsible for the administration and distribution of a special Sports Fund.

Article II of the Charter touches on resources – specifically financial – stating that 'Sport shall be encouraged as an important factor in human development, and appropriate support shall be made available out of public funds'.

If efforts to promote *Sport for All* were to be successful, more funds had to be pumped in: the Council of Europe's grant for 1977 from its general budget was manifestly inadequate. More resources were needed. Temporary provision was arranged pending acceptance by the Council of Europe of its full financial responsibility.

The special Sports Fund, set up in 1977, in fact stayed in balance until 1979, when Council of Europe appropriations[1] made it possible for member states' voluntary contributions to be discontinued. During the critical period, 1977–79, it was the extra million francs given in the form of national contributions, at rates based on those laid down for the Cultural Fund, that filled the coffers and made ends meet.

Initially the special fund was administered by a committee of senior officials which was also responsible for preparing documents for the Conference of Ministers for Sport, thus duplicating the work of the CDDS. By the London conference the matter was on the way to being resolved: the committee of senior officials effected a straightforward transfer of its management powers to the newly set up CDDS.

At their third conference in Palma de Majorca (1981), the Ministers for Sport returned to the main themes covered in London, noting that progress had been made:

'The end of the beginning has been reached; the CDDS is now firmly established, with its own identity, its own budget and its own programme. . . . In a time of economic pressure and high unemployment the case for sport and physical recreation has to be underlined and repeated often, as competing activities clamour for scarce resources. The progress described . . . should help those who have to argue this case'.

European co-operation had made progress on the themes studied at every informal meeting of sports ministers or their colleagues: in Paris (May 1978), Athens (March 1979) and Strasbourg (March 1980). The discussions and resolutions arising from these meetings related to problems of sport in society, especially the participation of target groups in sport, the sports sciences and human and ethical aspects of the practice of sport. Closer co-operation with member states' ministers for health was planned, with a view to providing medical cover for sportsmen. Mention was made of a willingness to liaise with the leaders of the Olympic movement (IOC) and with international sports federations (GAISF), and talks with them actually took place at Lisbon in October 1977, and subsequently at regular intervals.

In Malta in 1984, the sports ministers had before them a summary of all the studies and activities carried out by the CDDS in the past four years, chaired first by Helmut Emmerl (FRG) and then by Ferdinand Imesch (Switzerland), one representing a government body and the other a non-governmental organisation[2]. Details of the activities included will be dealt with later, but a random list of just a few of them will show the variety of areas in which European co-operation is possible: energy-saving measures, low-cost sports facilities, access to nature in mountain regions, sport for immigrants, sport for children, testing physical fitness, the challenge of increasing leisure time to sport and recreation policies, professional support of volunteers in sport, etc.

The fifth formal Conference of Ministers for Sport, in Dublin (1986), revealed co-operation to have reached maturity and to be capable of responding very rapidly – even immediately – to matters arising within its sphere of influence.

Following a settling down period and an exploratory phase, the

CDDS made use of its information centre, the Clearing House, to reach maximum efficiency in facing up to unexpected problems and in rapidly suggesting solutions and positions that the agencies of the Council of Europe could adopt.

As we have already pointed out, it was this policy of 'quick response' which was pursued in respect of violence at sports grounds, and it has also operated in reaction to the misuse of stimulants, leading to a continuously updated European Anti-doping Charter for Sport.

When European political bodies are one step ahead of international sports organisations, there may even be anticipation instead of reaction. The CDDS, at a seminar in Papendal (Netherlands) in 1986, prepared documents on 'new partnerships in sport' for the Dublin conference. These related to financial support from sponsors and the media. This study went further than any sports federation had yet gone: sports officials had been happy to observe and take advantage of this support, without analysing it. The CDDS, however, has already drawn up a clear policy on this development, which could have both the best and the worst possible consequences for sport:

> '*Sport is now dealing with new partners. Commercial interest (especially sponsorship) and media interest (particularly television exposure) offer new and different possibilities. The financial consequences of this involvement by media and sponsors are considered by sports organisations to be a useful contribution to the development of sport: for example in equipment, organisation and employment*'.

However, a warning is sounded immediately afterwards:

> '*Nevertheless the continuation of the basic balances in sport should be guaranteed, such as: the independence of the sports movement, protecting the ethics of sport (and) preserving the objectives of sport and respect of the athlete as an individual*'.

The CDDS report says that there could be a call for public authorities to take action if these balances were not maintained, but not until the sports officials had reacted, as 'primary responsibility for taking the lead in reacting to these developments lies with the sports organisations'.

In this specific and ultimately very typical case, the CDDS, thanks to smooth European co-operation, was able to play to the full its role as the 'voice of conscience', predicting and giving prior notice of certain trends which might improve or damage the development of sport.

Notes:

(1) Appropriations were doubled in 1979 (500,000F, compared to 230,000F in 1978), after which there were regular increases from 722,000F in 1980 to 1,220,000F in 1986. In the 8 years between 1978 and 1986, the Council of Europe's grant to sport increased more than fivefold.

(2) The first chairman of the CDDS was Sir Walter Winterbottom (United Kingdom, 1978) followed by Max Wasterlain (Belgium, 1979) and Wim van Zjill (Netherlands, 1980–81).

Sport's relationship with the social and the cultural

Sport must be careful not to become too self-centred. While it does essentially depend on itself and on its own organisation, vitality, initiative, achievements and even appropriate funding, it is not dependent solely on itself. The Council of Europe has recognised that sport has a degree of independence and given it freedom of action through the setting up of the CDDS, but points out that it remains linked to the socio-cultural family from which it stems.

Article III of the Charter emphasises this relationship, stating that sport is related 'to other areas of policy-making and planning'; the family's cousins, so to speak, are named: 'education, health, social services, town and country planning, conservation, the arts and leisure services'. But these 'cousins' are fairly often 'heads of family' in the area of sport and physical activities.

Luxembourg, Greece and France are virtually the only countries with a ministry or government department responsible solely for sport, and even in France sport is coupled with youth, and the ministry fairly recently expanded to cover all 'leisure' activities. Turkey combines education, youth and sport. Tourism and entertainment encompass sport in Italy, and it comes under the heading of welfare and health in the Netherlands and environment in the United Kingdom. The most common umbrellas, of course, are culture and education, and these cover sport in Denmark, Spain, Finland, Ireland, Iceland and Portugal. The Federal Republic of Germany and Switzerland place sport among the responsibilities of the interior ministry, and Sweden, less predictably, attaches sport to agriculture.

Obviously, these are all related to certain categories of sport or physical activity. Nowhere in the world can education ignore sport at schools and universities, defence fail to allow for sport in the army or labour pay no attention to sport or physical activity in the work context.

The environment ministries are concerned about access to nature, which is guaranteed by Article VII of the Charter:

'Measures, including legislation where appropriate, shall be introduced to ensure access to open country and water for the purpose of recreation'.

Forests, rivers, the sea, mountains and the countryside in general are all natural areas which are in demand for open air recreational activities and sports, and sometimes even for high level competition. The Council of Europe has recommended that governments ask their local, regional and national authorities to draw up unambiguous rules for their use, reconciling all the interests concerned. This amounts to saying that freedom of access to these areas must be absolutely guaranteed, where they are publicly or privately owned[1].

Schemes have been launched in every country, and some nations have had to pass legislation, as disputes about wooded and mountainous areas and stretches of water have been common. Hence the Deutscher Sportbund's declaration that, in principle 'sport and the environment are indivisible', and its detailed research, some carried out at Lower Saxony's Landessportbund congress (October 1985), culminating in the drafting of a code of conduct which lays down that sports training must include instruction about the environment[2].

Most frequently it is sports bodies which have made the necessary efforts to instil discipline. An example is the Swiss Association for Sport, which has set down rules for the sympathetic use of woodland, as it tries to bring about dialogue and mutual understanding between owners and users (ie visitors and tourists). The former have agreed not to prohibit access, while the latter have undertaken not to harm flora and fauna.

Where *Sport for All* is linked to social affairs and health, the subjects covered are family sport, holiday sport and sport as a means to achieve health and well-being. There is no shortage of practical manifestations of this, and they do have some success. Austrian women appreciate 'mother and child' or 'couples' (Er und Sie) exercise classes. Luxembourg holds a festival of sport (Fete sportive/ Spillcfest) to promote family sport (Sport en famille/Sport Mit der Familie), and Swiss citizens are invited to share sporting and family events 'En famille sur le parcours Vita' (with the family on the Vita track)[3].

In the Federal Republic of Germany, the Federal Committee for Popular Sport (Bundesausschuss fur Breitensport) is motivated by the same spirit in its 'shared activity' (Miteinander aktiv) campaign, which encourages people to engage in sport with members of their families, friends and neighbours, as the Swedes do in the neighbour-

23

hood sports events arranged as part of their 'Togetherness' movement.

Activity or sporting holidays are now fashionable in various European and other countries. Austria's 'walking shoes' programme, mountain holiday courses in the United Kingdom and the Federal Republic of Germany's 'Kiel holiday passport' make holidays possible for social classes to which they were previously unknown[4], but fashions also entail a certain amount of snobbery and commercial exploitation. People book expensive, tiring courses in sports for the well-to-do (tennis, sailing, golf, etc) in the same way as they book holiday trips.

Finally, sport is undoubtedly vital to health. It is even important to national budgets. It is understandable that Austria is being encouraged to continue its 'Health and Nutrition' campaign through the BSO (Bundes-Sportorganisation), in co-operation with sports federations. A similar campaign is running in Finland, sponsored over three years by the food industry. In the Netherlands, the National Institute for Sportsmen's Health took more cautious action in 1985, based on the theme: 'Sport is good, but prevention better' (Sport is Goed, Preventie Moet). The Federal Republic of Germany's catch phrases are: 'Sport is good for you' and 'the best remedy is movement' (Bewegung ist die beste Medizin). The aim is to make people aware of the beneficial, measurable effects of sport on health and to involve in the crusade both the press and doctors who are asked to recommend that their adult patients between 30 and 60 take care of their joints, arteries and muscles by taking up 'Trimming 130' (a type of recreational sport activity).

France uses similar terms: its slogan is 'Make a move for Health' (Bougez-vous la santé). France's first woman minister for sport, Edwige Avice said 'Sportez-vous bien' (play sport to keep fit), based on 'portez-vous bien' ('keep health', and the English 'sport'). The language of sport too, clearly benefits from European co-operation.

Notes:

(1) Work was done on this at the seminars at Wilhelminaoord (Netherlands) in 1980 and Mont-Dauphin (France) in 1982.

(2) The German report was looked at again by the formal Conference of Ministers for Sport in Dublin, in 1986.

(3) *Vita* is a life assurance company which sponsors these events.

(4) Statistics have shown that, after the 'Sport during the Holidays' campaign in France, juvenile delinquency decreased markedly at centres where games and sports had been available for adolescents who were not going on holiday.

Technical and economic assistance and help from the media

While it is appropriate for sport to cultivate good relations and engage in joint action with the socio-cultural sphere (Article III), the Charter also recommends fostering 'permanent and effective co-operation between public authorities and voluntary organisations' (Article IV).

Sport could not survive without its voluntary workers. Its greatest asset is its leaders' devotion. Volunteers take responsibility at every level of the workings of associations, federations, leagues and clubs. It is up to those who are elected to define and implement policy and to determine how the sport is run.

What the Council of Europe wishes to avoid above all is the creation of conflict between voluntary organisers and sports officials or paid experts. Article IV takes every precaution, stating that each government 'shall encourage the establishment of national machinery for the development and co-ordination of *Sport for All*'.

The comments on this article mention the need for partnership and a strong and flexible administrative structure of the kind most appropriate to each country's circumstances. The structures referred to vary widely from country to country. In some cases they are solely government responsibilities, in others government representatives are involved, as they are in certain sports federations, while other countries have completely different systems. However, all bodies with an interest in sport ought at least to be made aware of the *Sport for All* concept.

Federations responsible for popular sports which attract spectators and media coverage are often reluctant to respond to insistent appeals for co-operation to encourage people to participate in a different kind of sport, whose educational value and social significance they do not appreciate. Realising that these obstacles lay ahead, the Council of Europe mapped out a cohesive course and has shown the foundations on which *Sport for All* could be organised.

A specific localised example is the 'Fete des Jeux' (Gamesfestival) in the province of Aquitaine in south-western France, which regularly attracts 5 to 10 thousand people to one place (a town or village) to take part in sports and recreational activities. This idea is fairly common in other countries too, such as Switzerland, the Federal Republic of Germany and Canada, with an additional 'folk' aspect emphasising regional identity and providing a new link with cultural traditions.

What is special about the French experience is the way in which it is organised. The initiative is taken by the 'Association Aquitaine Sport pour Tous', a private, voluntary body which plans, makes the arrangements for and runs the event with the assistance of the regional offices of the Ministry for Youth and Sport and CROS (Regional Olympic and Sports Committee) officials; thus both the government and a local sports body give their help. The municipality provides the facilities, local clubs look after the technical arrangements, the town's schools encourage and facilitate participation by their pupils, the south-western regional press and television (FR3 Bordeaux) provide an information service and the Credit Mutuel (a regional bank) helps with the funding.

We have not yet considered the funding of *Sport for All* campaigns and events. As we have already seen, the development of the sports sector necessitated increased appropriations from the Council of Europe and even support from a Special Fund for the setting up of international co-ordination machinery. In every country there is the same pressing need, nationally and at regional and local levels, for more funding if all forms of sport and every kind of sporting event are to be properly promoted.

The Clearing House statistics for Council of Europe member states show the highest percentage of general national budgets allocated to sport usually to be around 0.2%. It is difficult to be sure of the figures, however, as not all the sectors covered by the budget grant are shown separately. The Federal Republic of Germany's figure is over 3%, but this is for health and recreation as well as sport, and the Netherlands budget of 0.6% is three times higher than that of France, but in fact constitutes the budget for the Ministry of Welfare and Health. The European Charter claims a share for *Sport for All*. Do not forget that Article II itself is a call for state cash: 'appropriate support shall be made available out of public funds' for the promotion of sport.

A CDDS report on sport and local authorities[1] is even more categorical, saying that sport 'should be considered as a *public service*' and to be funded by local authorities, with the help of state subsidies. It also said that a modest contribution from the users to the cost of sports facilities 'may be seen to be appropriate'. The CDDS used a political argument to justify its demand for local authority funding, saying that the development of sport was one of the main ways of improving the quality of life in a community, thus strengthening people's attachment to the area. It also fostered mutual understanding.

*Economic arguments may also be put forward, as they were at the international colloquy in Bordeaux[2] by Jurgen Palm, a German, and Nigel Hook, of the United Kingdom, who revealed the effects of *Sport for All* on the economy and on the sports goods market. Dr. Jean-Claude Labadie added his view:

> 'It is high time that the sport movement cast off its image of dependency on the begging bowl and on various subsidies. It must demonstrate that the millions of active sportsmen are major cogs in their nations' economic machinery'.

*The state and regional and local authorities also recover from sport some of the subsidies they give it. The Treasury collects entertainment tax and the taxes paid on purchases of sports equipment, the construction of sports facilities and the many varied economic activities connected with sport. And while some of the profits from football pools and similar competitions go to help sport and sportsmen, the state is ultimately the greatest beneficiary. Those who drafted the European Charter were aware of all these considerations, and, despite its importance, couched the recommendation below in subtle terms:

> 'It is . . . the purpose of this document . . . to argue that there is public responsibility to support the Sport for All programmes and to emphasise that it cannot be successfully comprehensive unless that responsibility is acknowledged and generously acted upon'.

*Nevertheless, we ought not to rely solely on the public authorities' generosity. Technical co-operation with private organisations or sponsors may be combined with financial assistance. The CDDS opened the way to this in 1983, when it published the European Sports Sponsorship Code, a document aimed at national sports organisations and offering guidelines for the conclusion of sponsorship agreements between them and private partners offering financial assistance.

Contracts with sponsors are not contracts with the devil. Back in 1981, a CDDS report presented by Andre van Lierde to the ICSPE (International Council for Sport and Physical Education) reached the interesting conclusion that promoting *Sport for All* required a number of techniques from the world of commerce (advertising, product distribution, price policy, etc), but that one essential fact fortunately distinguished *Sport for All* from a commercial activity: in the former, it was the consumer who benefited, not the producer.

The European Sports Sponsorship Code, which was aimed at sport-for-all organisations and approved by the Ministers for Sport at their Palma conference in 1981, deserves to be better known by certain sports federations. It refers to the 'important, indeed vital, contribution' made by sportsmen. They are the ones who actually compete and provide entertainment. The media, particularly television, are stated to be among the essential partners. All the media publicise events, promoting them and making the public familiar with them. Television broadcasts, especially, foster the image of an event's sponsor or sponsors and sports events provide the press as a whole with an inexhaustible supply of news to comment on, emotions to convey and pictures to record.

The CDDS does not wish to see government intervention in these three-way agreements unless they get out of control or break the law. Its constant concern is to safeguard the authenticity and ethics of sport.

The CDDS held a series of seminars between 1975 and 1977, organised by Norway in conjunction with Greece and the Federal Republic of Germany; their theme was 'the role of television in promoting the practice of sport' and they culminated in a recommendation to governments adopted by the Committee of Ministers on 'Sport and Television'.

Notes:

(1) Seminar held in Madrid by the Spanish Supreme Sports Council (24–26 April 1979).

(2) 3rd international *Sport for All* colloquy, Bordeaux (7–8 November 1986).

(3) Seminar held in Papendal (Netherlands) by the Netherlands Ministry of Welfare and Health and for Cultural Affairs (22–24 April 1986).

Protecting sport from politics, money, violence and doping

While the state should assist sport, especially for social and humane reasons, there is also a state duty to protect sport from itself – from its own excesses, or its exploitation and compromises and any tendency to stray from its path. Article V of the *Sport for All* Charter says:

> '*Methods shall be sought to safeguard sport and sportsmen from exploitation for political, commercial or financial gain, and from practices that are abusive and debasing, including the unfair use of drugs*'.

The four targets of this text are politics and money on the one hand, and violence and doping on the other.

1. Politics

Politics is a dangerous game, even for people who condemn it: it is difficult for them to obtain a real consensus in areas where political intentions, however laudable, are involved.

The Council of Europe denounces any damaging interference in sport and all forms of discrimination. Hence its logical opposition to apartheid and anti-semitism in sport. However, while they may be in complete agreement about the basic issue and principles, governments and sports organisations – which do not have the same kind of responsibilities – are far less inclined to adopt common tactics or the same attitude as each other. At the Dublin Conference of Ministers for Sport, unanimity was not achieved on the resolution against apartheid or the call to break all sports links with South Africa[1].

The problem arose in similar terms in relation to the Moscow

29

Olympics in 1980: the Council of Europe was never able to persuade all member states to adopt the same attitude. From January 1980 onwards, the Council of Europe's Parliamentary Assembly brought maximum pressure to bear on member states' Olympic Committees, asking them to reconsider participation in the light of events in Afghanistan. Not every member bowed to this pressure, and the sports community went against government advice in some countries (especially France, the United Kingdom, Portugal and Luxembourg).

In December 1980, after the boycott of the Moscow Games by three Council of Europe members' Olympic Committees (Federal Republic of Germany, Norway and Turkey), the Assembly expressed approval of the idea of setting up a permanent site for the games near Olympia, and the Assembly's Committee on Culture asked the former French minister, Maurice Druon, to carry out a study which was never followed up: the IOC does not intend to allow itself to be swayed.

Even before Moscow and the Afghanistan affair, the Ministers for Sport had declared at their 1979 meeting in Athens that they would like to see a limit to the use of national anthems and flags in order to avoid stirring up nationalist passions.

Ministers and members of the Assembly are powerless to restrict political influence on sport, since they are themselves politicians, and while they can always condemn such influence, it would be very risky to try to codify it. Could any convention prevent a Head of State, a minister, a member of a regional assembly or a town mayor from congratulating and flattering a national, regional or local champion in an attempt to gain some slight political advantage? Acclaim for the winner is, within reason, a normal part of the celebration of victory[2] but how can sport be prevented from becoming totally subservient to a political system?

2. The question of money

The practice and development of sport requires money, as do sports facilities and training for officials and for top flight athletes. According to *Sport for All* doctrine, money for sport from the state or local communities must be used for this purpose and no other. If such money is used to promote a commercial event which neither boosts the practice of, nor promotes, a sport or sport in general, it is being misused. Sport also generates some money itself and attracts more through its commercial, advertising and media potential.

The Council of Europe adopts a cautious approach to this aspect of sport. It can always carry out studies and issue advice and recommendations, but it cannot impose rules or any form of control. The European Sports Sponsorship Code[3] bears witness to this.

Each member state has its own safeguards against the misuse of sport as an advertising vehicle. Some countries ban alcohol and tobacco products from sports grounds and competitions. The EBU (European Broadcasting Union) has laid down nine principles to prevent excessive advertising during television screening of international sports events[4].

The Council of Europe does what it can in this area, trying to inject positive ethics into relations between sport and money, but however great its moral authority, it does not have the muscle of economic forces like the McCormack group (representing professional sportsmen) and advertising companies and agencies with exclusive contracts with the IOC.

3. Violence

Is violence part and parcel of sport? Is it a product of society? Or is man just naturally violent? No other subject has spawned so many colloquies, debates, conferences and studies or called upon the services of so many sociologists, psychologists, doctors, legal experts, academics, managers and journalists.

Only one thing is certain: violence has chosen sport in general and certain sports grounds in particular as an arena for its unrestricted expression – thereby damaging sport (which is sometimes a guilty party, but more frequently a victim). Yet it is sport, in its educational role, which ought to be holding violence in check if we are to believe Ernest Gilbert's elegant statement that 'since it is the means of transforming selfishness into solidarity, sport must enable man to set aside his own violence'[5].

Violence in sport[6] has caused too much damage and had too many victims not to require solidarity among states themselves. The Council of Europe has clearly understood this, and had embarked upon a crusade against violence well before the Heysel stadium tragedy. This explains the speed and effectiveness of its response. The European Convention on Spectator Violence, which came into force at the end of 1985, is more than a statement of intent. Its 16 detailed articles suggest possible government action, including remedial action, in respect of monitoring, prevention, education and, if necessary, enforcement. Moreover, all states with teams in football competitions must, as agreed with UEFA, make their own arrangements and draw up their own rules. (For a history of the Convention, see the end of this chapter.)

4. Doping

Doping is a danger to both health and dignity. In 1981 the Olympic

31

1,500 metres champion, Sebastian Coe, went even further, telling the Olympic congress in Baden-Baden that athletes believed doping to be the 'most shameful abuse of the Olympic idea' and called for athletes who took drugs to be banned for life, along with the 'coaches and so-called doctors who administer this evil'.

Doping has several features in common with violence. Is it not violence against one's own person, against nature and against the rules, in order to contrive a result? Doping, like violence, is not confined to sport; it is practised in other social contexts and, by another name, is infiltrating the younger generation.

The Council of Europe followed the same pattern for doping as for violence, convening its group of experts, chaired by the Prince of Merode and liaising with the work of the IOC's Medical Commission and of international federations, via the GAISF[7]. It had a survey conducted through the Clearing House into the rules introduced, measures adopted, needs experienced and difficulties encountered by 21 international federations and by 16 member states. The findings were analysed, and the process got under way with a resolution by a Conference of Sport Ministers and the approval of the Charter by the Committee of Ministers.

The latter document is there for governments to use; it strengthens essential measures – legislative, enforcement and educational – gives encouragement to research in analytical chemistry and biochemistry, specifies methods of monitoring doping, suggests that laboratories be set up to detect prohibited products and lays down penalties.

Like the convention on violence, the anti-doping charter has both a punitive and an educational side. But punitive measures are not taken lightly, and at their Dublin conference in 1986 the Ministers for Sport were anxious to increase the rights of athletes suspected of doping: the ministers demanded that such athletes should have a 'fair hearing' and be guaranteed the right to appeal to a higher body in their own sport, so that the relevant personal circumstances would be taken into account. Their concern was not only for detail, but also, primarily, for justice.

The history of the Convention on Spectator Violence

September 1977:   The two Belgian Ministers, Rika de Backer-Van Ocken (Dutch Culture) and Jean-Maurice Dehousse (French Culture) invited representatives of Council of Europe member states and various individuals to Brussels to attend a congress on violence in sport.

April 1978:   The Ministers responsible for Sport, at their second

32

conference in London, adopted a resolution expressing their determination to take action against violence.

January 1983:
In Paris Neil Macfarlane, the United Kingdom Minister for Sport, suggested to his colleagues that joint precautions against violence in football grounds be studied.

June 1983:
The Parliamentary Assembly recommended that a European Convention on Violence be drawn up. At that point, the CDDS set up a working party, chaired by David Teasdale (United Kingdom), which established links with the Rika de Backer-Van Ocken Foundation and UEFA (Union of European Football Associations).

March 1984:
The recommendation submitted to the Committee of Ministers was approved and sent to member states' governments.

17 May 1985:
At their Lisbon meeting, the Ministers responsible for Sport asked the CDDS to study the initial effects of the recommendation.

29 May 1985:
Thirty-nine people died in the Heysel stadium tragedy.

June 1985:
The CDDS working party drafted a convention, which was considered and adopted at its third reading at the Strasbourg meeting of Sport Ministers, prior to submission to the Committee of Ministers.

July 1985:
The European Convention on spectator violence and misbehaviour at sports events and in particular at football matches was adopted by the Committee of Ministers.

August 1985:
The convention was opened for signature by member states; application was to start that very year.

July 1986:
First meeting, in Strasbourg, of the Standing Committee (established by the Convention). The Committee elected David Teasdale chairman and assessed the early positive effects of the Convention.

The history of the European Anti-doping Charter for Sport

1960:
The Council of Europe condemned the effects of doping.

1967:	The Committee of Ministers adopted its first resolution on the subject.
1975:	Article V of the *Sport for All* Charter stipulated that methods should be sought to protect sportsmen from 'abusive and debasing' practices.
1978:	Resolution at the London conference of ministers on the dangers of doping.
1979:	The above resolution became a Committee of Ministers recommendation.
1982–83:	A group of experts set up by the CDDS prepared the text of the charter.
1984:	Following examination by the Malta conference of Ministers for Sport, the charter was adopted in September by the Committee of Ministers, which made it into a recommendation to member states.
1988:	Recommendation adopted by the Committee of Ministers on Doping Controls without warning for outside competition.
Comments:	Doubtless because of the number of cycle races in Belgium and France, those two countries had been the first to legislate to prohibit doping (in 1965). The first official drug tests were conducted by the IOC at the 1968 Winter Olympics, in Grenoble.

Notes:

(1) France abstained. The explanation given to the French press by Christian Bergelin, Secretary of State for Sport, was that the matter was more one of politics than sport.

(2) Especially, in team sports, at the post-match celebration.

(3) See Chapter 6.

(4) Outside Europe, and especially when broadcasts come from Eastern bloc nations, television companies and sponsors from member states readily forget about the EBU's principles.

(5) Professor Ernest Gilbert (University of Rouen) put forward this view to the young sportsmen from the Federal Republic of Germany, the United Kingdom and France who attended the 'Sport and Violence' colloquy at Marly-le-Roi (France) in December 1986.

(6) Three international associations have joined forces in the face of the rising tide of violence in sport: the AICVS (International Committee Against Violence in

Sport), which is supported by Prince Rainier of Monaco; the International Fair Play Committee, led by Jean Borotra; and the International Foundation Rika de Backer-Van Ocken for the Fight Against Violence associated with Sport. The De Backer foundation launched a 'Fair Play, OK' campaign in Flanders which ran from October 1986 to Easter 1987, during which time it supplied teachers with written material in Dutch enabling them to draw their pupils' attention to fair play.

(7) The General Association of International Sports Federations.

Research and communication

Research

Solutions to political, technical, sociological, physiological, medical and human problems are not easily found – they have to be actively sought. The CDDS and its predecessor, the CDS, have accordingly made it a constant practice to call on the opinion of experts and thus, researchers.

This was first done via the heads of research institutes in the member states. They held nine meetings in all in a bid for coordination, and were helped in this by the heads of the Information Relay Centres, who between 1972 and 1979 held four meetings. Then, on 13 October 1980 the Committee of Experts on Sports Research (DS–SR) was officially established.

Since then, the DS–SR, which meets annually and elects a new Chairman every year[1], has formed the research unit of the CDDS. It collaborates closely with the Committee whose main activities it guides and channels, supplying references, reports, surveys and food for thought generally.

A glimpse at the minutes of its various meetings reveals, for instance, the contribution of the Research Committee in the choice of the EUROFIT tests. As early as the first meeting in 1980, Michael Collins, of the UK – following suggestions from Claude Adam (France) to the effect that there should be a European project on physical fitness and an initial INSEP seminar in 1978 – reported on the findings of the 2nd Seminar held in Birmingham on 'testing physical fitness'; Professor Vassilis Klissouras (Greece) presented a paper on standard ways of testing the physical work capacity of young people between the ages of 6 and 18, and Professor Roland Renson (Belgium) reported that a further seminar was to be held in

36

Leuven, in order to devise a battery of tests on motor aspects. Two years later, the experts on sports research were able to submit a preliminary draft recommendation on EUROFIT (see following chapter) to the CDDS.

The fact of being able to bring together researchers, information specialists, decision-takers and 'doers' is one of the major assets of the Council of Europe, and it makes the process of co-ordination that much more effective.

One of the main areas of research of the DS–SR is on the rationalisation of sports policies. The title may appear obscure but the aim of the survey was to make a study of sports participation in a number of member countries[2]. In May 1982, with the simplified title 'Sport in European Society' the CDDS published in two volumes the findings of this transnational survey entrusted to Urbain Claeys[3], based on the earlier work of Benito Castejon (1973) and Brian Rodgers (1977).

It is not so up-to-date as it was, being based on data for 1979, but its methodology still holds good for indicating and even measuring a nation's participation in physical activity and its motivation. Some facts and figures are still significant and relevant.

A first general finding: the average rate of casual participation in sport works out at a steady 70% in the member states. The highest rate is in Sweden (98%), followed by Denmark and urban areas of Flanders (90%); yet the figure for continuous practice of sport never exceeds 50%, with the highest rates in Flanders (45%), the United

Formulae for measuring the practice of sport

Penetration	:	*Those having ever practised a sport*
		Total population
Participation	:	*Number of active practitioners*
		Total population
Fidelity	:	*Number of active practitioners*
		Number of still active practitioners and those having ever practised a sport
Differentiation Index		Total number of hours devoted to sport each year
		....
		Number of sports practitioners

Kingdom (42%), followed by France (36%), and the lowest figure for Denmark (28%) and Sweden (15%).

The most eclectic among the sport-active are the British and the Swedes, who engage in up to 10 different sports, while the French and Germans content themselves with two or three, although they devote more time to those sports they have opted for. The most widely practised sports are individual ones: walking and swimming, followed by cycling (non-competitive), fishing and hunting. Team sports, such as football, volley ball and netball also present good rates.

The last part of the survey deals with the strongest influences in motivating people towards participation; these include natural, geographical, climatic and environmental conditions. Nautical sports are more popular in countries bordering the sea, downhill skiing in mountainous countries, and cross-country skiing in Scandinavian countries. Socio-structural and cultural factors are also at work: age, education, occupation and sex all have an effect. Friends, partners, workmates and parents are the most significant influences in either encouraging or discouraging the taking up of a sport.

Communication

Motivation – and this is something the Council of Europe cannot afford to neglect – can be encouraged by a well-planned and well publicised sports policy. We know from experience that the basic factor in the decision not to continue a sport is a social or family reason. All too often people give up sport when they leave school.

It was noted in January 1984, on the occasion of a DS–SR meeting on the 'Evaluation of the impact of *Sport for All* policies and programmes' in Dudzele, in the Flemish community of Belgium, that in almost all countries the lower social classes have very low participation rates compared with national overall rates. The same meeting discussed the role of the media and reports showed that television was a powerful means for conveying information but that it had not been very effectively used to date for leisure. Clearly, it was *a priori* devoted to competitive sport and sport as an entertainment, but the DS–SR hoped that the media, like sports organisations, would cover both competitive and recreational sports.

Sports policy on a European scale needs communication to sustain and shore it up if it is to work – and that means first and foremost its own communication. The Council of Europe has an information centre, via the CDDS, for familiarising people with its policies and actions, disseminating its thinking and promoting measures to apply for everyone's benefit. It also serves as an information centre on the activities, initiatives and experiments going on in the different member states. That centre is the Clearing House.

Sport bridges the generation gap.

Enjoying sport in the open air.

Getting together over a game.

Exploring the countryside.

The Vasaloppet, a 70 km cross-country skiing race, attracts 70,000 people.

Italian and Portuguese sports posters.

Sport can help make society less violent.

Sport without violence.

Sport for all has social and cultural implications.

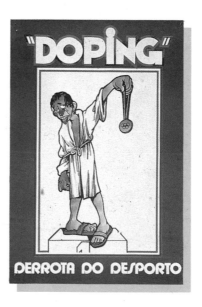

Anti-doping.

Sport and health, Portuguese poster.

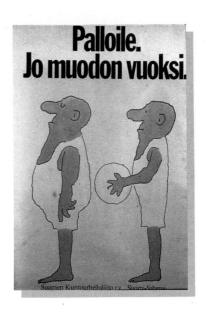

Keep fit, Finnish poster.

Sport begins with physical education at school, Belgian poster.

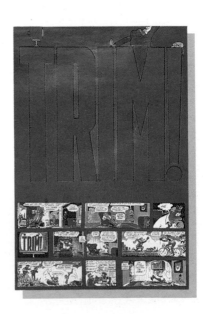

Keep fit, Norwegian poster.

Get in training for the sports
diplomas, German poster.

Recreational sports festival for
all ages, Germany.

Respect nature, Swedish poster.

Council of Europe leaders'
training course, Portuguese
poster.

Outdoor recreation and training for young people.

Youth games festival.

Sport is best, Belgian poster.

Council of Europe sticker and posters.

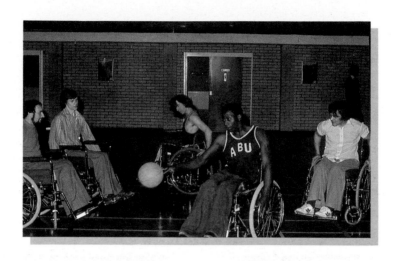

Many people with disabilities now enjoy sport.

As long ago as 1966, when *Sport for All* was first being promoted, people realised the need for an international exchange of information. The first attempt was distinctly improvised, and the resulting failure prompted Armand Lams (Belgium), Franz Holzweber (Austria) and Jurgen Palm (Federal Republic of Germany), meeting in Oslo in 1969, to seek a specialised structure to meet this need. It was not so much ideas that were wanting as resources. Thus, the offer made by the Dutch-speaking Minister of Culture, Frans Van Mechelen and his French-speaking opposite number, Albert Parisis, to set up an information service on *Sport for All* in Belgium and to be responsible for it, was welcomed with open arms. And so the Clearing House came into being[4].

Its admission, not to say its integration, into the Council of Europe was in accordance with the rules: first, adoption by the Committee on Culture and Education in September 1971, and then recognition by the Committee of Ministers in January 1972. Its own identity and its legal existence in the host country were established when the Clearing House adopted legal statutes consistent with Belgian law, and become a non-profit-making association administered by a 12-member board of directors[5]. By September 1974 the Clearing House was settled in its own headquarters, provided by the Belgian French-speaking community in the heart of Brussels.

The Executive Director of the Clearing House has described the way in which it operates as follows: its principal concern is information rather than documentation. 'From the outset, the Clearing House has sent out a constant stream of information on the various developments in sport in the Council of Europe member countries. Between 1974 and 1985 this was done through analytical data cards, dealing with over 1,400 topics. Since June 1985 the data cards have been superseded by a Sports Information Bulletin in the form of a loose-leaf folder. The Bulletin features both brief reports from different countries (an extension as it were of the data cards), and also summary reports on priority topics in sports policy.'

The Clearing House also brings out occasional comparative studies, eg on topics for European seminars (such as sport at school, doping, the planning of sports facilities in times of economic recession), and practical booklets (abbreviations used in sport, the way sport is organised in the Council of Europe member states). Since 1986 the CDDS indicates its priority topics for information exchange each year and asks the Clearing House to carry out the appropriate investigations in the member countries.

A network of persons to provide the Clearing House with this information is needed: from 1975 onwards, use was made of 'liaison officers' (correspondents appointed by each country), subsequently called the 'Sports Information Officers'. This network of persons providing and disseminating information was replaced in 1987 by a committee of information experts (DS–SI), the counterpart of the committee of research experts (DS–SR). The DS–SI held its first meeting in Strasbourg in May 1987. Members are required to assemble information and documentation so as to make it easier for information to be exchanged through the Clearing House.

The information provided by experts and processed by the Clearing House is principally intended for members of the CDDS, but it is also available to other decision-takers and any persons who are interested; they can ask for it or take out a subscription to the Bulletins.

Up until 1985 the Clearing House was both a centre for information on *Sport for All* policies and at the same time a centre for research information. From 1975 onwards, it was involved in listing the sports research projects underway in Council of Europe member countries.

The Federal Institute for Sports Sciences in Cologne published the first inventory of these research projects (1976–1977). A fuller and more effective use of the information assembled in the inventory meant computerisation: the CDDS experimented with its own data bank, and, at the instigation of the Project Director, Andre van Lierde, an experimental project was put in hand in 1980. Close on 3,000 research projects were fed into the computer during the experimental phase. For a variety of reasons, the central data bank in Brussels ceased, and to ensure continuity the data bank has been split between four regional centres since 1986. The Federal Institute of Sports Science in Cologne, Federal Republic of Germany; the National Institute of Physical Education and Sport (INSEP) in France; the Italian National Olympic Committee (CONI); and the Sports Council in the United Kingdom have undertaken to continue the sports research data bank.

The Clearing House, relying on the DS–SR and DS–SI and propagating information through them, itself encourages co-operation in the Council of Europe. Not surprising, then, that its important role is reflected in the Third Medium-Term Plan (1987–1991): 'Another element . . . is the need to exploit and develop the achievements of the past, notably by sharing information, research results and experience in a wide variety of more technical fields'.

Notes:

(1) 1980: Michael Collins (United Kingdom) and Claude Adam (France).
1981: Roland Renson (Belgium) – 1982: August Kirsch (Federal Republic of Germany) – 1983: Vassilis Klissouras (Greece) – 1984: Captain Michael McDonough (Ireland) – 1985: ABA Kemper (Netherlands) – 1986: Hélène Levarlet-Joye (Belgium).

(2) Nine countries took part in the project. Belgium, Denmark, Federal Republic of Germany, Great Britain, France, Greece, Portugal, Spain and Sweden. The survey covered populations between the ages of 14 and 65 years.

(3) Lecturer at the University of Leuven. The first survey (by Brian Rodgers, and published in 1977) ws encouraged by Gerard Herberichs, who was in charge of the sports section at the Council of Europe at the time.

(4) The Clearing House is an information centre for the planning and implementation of *Sport for All*. The headquarters of the Clearing House are in the Galerie Ravenstein 4–27, 1000 Brussels (telephone: 02–513.51.64).

(5) Its Board of Directors consist of six representatives from Belgium and six representatives of the Council of Europe, including the Chairman of the CDDS and the representative of the Secretary General. Its financing is provided by Belgium and the Council of Europe; a part of its income derives from the sale of publications.

9

Make way for women and children

If *Sport for All* can take as its slogan the expression 'make way for women and children', it is perhaps because although they have not been totally ignored, women and children only find a place in high-level and medium-level competitive sports if they can produce results. That is the way of things in sport, and there is also the weight of tradition whereby sport, like war, is an activity reserved for hale and hearty males. The prejudices of several generations had to be overcome before women could be released from the kitchen sink and encouraged to enter into the sports stadium or even into recreation, thus enabling them to share the leisure activities of their families.

Sportswomen belonging to a federation account for a mere 7% of the total number of women[1] and as registered players they tend to engage in team sports (volleyball, handball, hockey and football) and mainly in winter or recreation sports as individuals. However, even if the percentage of women registered in organised sports is still relatively low, the signs are that in all the Council of Europe member countries women's sport has expanded markedly over the last 20 years. Women have been able to discover for themselves that physical activity helps towards a better life, and brings valuable personal benefits. Though they may not be ardent participants in the official sports movement, women, if they can afford it, go swimming for pleasure almost as much as men (42% compared with 58%) and play tennis (41% compared with 59%). More women than men do traditional gymnastics, and far more women engage in movement and dance, keep fit classes etc. A recent survey carried out in France, and doubtless applicable to other countries, shows the astonishing recent development of gymnastics. Initially a military training activity and subsequently a popular school sport, particularly for

42

boys, women's gymnastics really took off in the early 1970s. Amongst the factors at work is certainly that of the influence of *Sport for All*, but we should also remember the noticeably higher level of women's emancipation since 1968, higher living standards, the opening of private centres, the building of local authority sports halls open to all, and encouragement by teachers of physical education and dance. Lastly, and this is something that is inherent in the philosophy of *Sport for All*, physical activity encourages the quest by women today for health and grace.

The CDDS seminar organised with the Irish Department of Education in October 1980 in Dublin took note of a real and profound change in attitudes towards a greater involvement by women in all aspects of sport. Experts at the seminar rejected the idea that exclusively female sports activities should be developed, but called for a legal guarantee of women's right to engage in sport – which suggests that this right does not yet exist in all countries, or that it has not yet become operational.

Is sport hostile to women or, being on the whole conservative and rooted in tradition, just hostile to innovation? Or does it merely reflect the attitudes of those in charge? In any event, the CDDS demands that women shall be associated with decision-taking concerning them, and shall have access to managerial posts in national and international sports organisations. Some governments have had to introduce decrees calling for women to be represented in the management of sports federations for mixed disciplines. An attempt was made at the seminar in Dublin to get to grips with the problem, calling on the media to see that women cover sports events at national and international level, 'even when they are mass spectator sports played by men'. There has been progress here in the last few years, but not enough – the sporting press is on the whole not sympathetic[3].

Make way for children – well, yes! The principle has been observed by the Council of Europe sports bodies, and the list of seminars concerned with physical education and sport for children of pre-school and post-school age[4] bears eloquent witness to the concern aroused by the subject, particularly in the CDDS. A start was made in Paris as early as 1976: based on the syllabuses, and on the physical education activities practised in the 11 member countries taking part in the seminar, priorities were determined to promote such action as was necessary.

Taking as its starting-point the idea that practising a sport is a dimension of human life, the seminar propounded the view that this should start as soon as the family is created, and continue at school. The environment should also be appropriate, with toys, space, partners and relationships. School gives the child time for sports activities and offers facilities close by. Sport makes for a child's sense of well-being in school and away from school, preparing him morally

43

and physically for adult life.

This basic work was taken a stage further a year later in Nice, and the following year in Luxembourg. The final report covered all aspects, including teacher training and specialist teacher training[5]. The report calls for mixed physical education classes, urging the competent authorities to encourage 'teachers of both sexes to teach mixed classes'.

It also stressed the change in direction advocated by the CDDS experts, who felt that excessive emphasis had been placed in schools so far on competitive sport; physical education should concentrate more on encouraging leisure-time sports. Similarly, educationalists were urged to pay more attention to less gifted and less motivated pupils, i.e. those most in need of encouragement to exert themselves physically, and to discover its benefits. The following comment puts this preoccupation in a nutshell: 'school sporting activities are so important in education as a whole that all categories of children, some of whom have been neglected in certain countries, must have the chance to participate'.

The seminar held in Tønsberg, Norway, on 'Sport for Children', which was particularly concerned with competition, was the occasion for warnings of all kinds against intensive and inappropriate training. A programme geared, for example, to physical strength training is liable to damage bone-growth areas in children, and should therefore be very moderate before puberty. Another comment – an obvious one, but one that needs to be remembered – is that competitions must be organised with the children's good in mind, not the pleasure of adults. There is no reason why they should not compete at club level, but immense caution is called for if children are allowed to compete at national or international level.

The educational role of sport is vital and it is in school that the education of the future athlete, spectator and supporter should begin. Children should be made to understand that while victory is the natural goal of competition, the spirit of sport also includes knowing how to cope with defeat.

Throughout the 23 countries which have acceded to the European Cultural Convention, there are 70 million children of school age. Do they receive satisfactory physical education and sport at primary and then at secondary school? Not entirely, to judge from the findings of a comparative survey carried out in 1981 by the Clearing House in 25 countries – those of Europe plus Canada, the United States and Brazil. The shortfalls are the same everywhere: not enough hours for physical education; in both schools and clubs the emphasis is on results and performance, and too infrequently on a sense of fair play, respect for the opponent and umpire. Television is so dominated by the elite that the child's idea of sporting achievement is distorted, and the sporting press is not geared to education.

Out-of-school efforts designed to supplement physical education in

44

small classes, well organised in some countries, need in view of the CDDS to be extended and developed at the adolescent stage. The theme and preoccupations of the Stockholm Seminar (1978) provided encouragement for the study of social and financial measures to ensure that pupils leaving school and students leaving universities have opportunities to continue to practise a sport or sports. If throughout his years at school physical education has given a child a liking for sport, an understanding of what it is about and reasons for practising it, he will continue to do so as an adolescent and as an adult. But far too many young people give up sports activities when they leave school, for family and social reasons.

The Seminar in Bilbao in 1985 was devoted to the values and purposes of physical education, concluding that it satisfied children's basic needs[7]. It also considered general objectives and methodology before making an assessment. This is a good point to look at another study and another assessment – that of physical fitness – which led to the creation of EUROFIT.

EUROFIT is a term now common to all the Council of Europe member countries; it is the physical fitness test for young Europeans. It is practical, it is the same for all, and it is affordable. The sports research body set up by the CDDS recognised in 1977 the need for finding ways of testing the physical fitness of schoolchildren in Europe. The sets of tests used at that time in Canada and the United States provided a source of experience and inspiration, but Europe was determined to seek its own formula, and strove to do so at the seminars organised at INSEP, Paris (October 1978), at the University of Birmingham (June 1980) the Catholic University of Leuven (May 1981), and the International Olympic Academy (May 1982). At this last, an experimental series of tests were devised and then tried out in 15 countries, before being reviewed and extended at the Seminar in Formia organised in May 1986 by the Italian National Olympic Committee (CONI). They assumed their present form and were recognised in May 1987 with the adoption of Recommendation R (87) 9 of the Committee of Ministers.

EUROFIT is indisputably one of the best reference points for the CDDS for reasons which are all very much bound up with the spirit of the Council of Europe. It symbolises and personifies the alliance of health, physical education and sport. It is useful for everybody:

- for the young undergoing the tests (between the age of 6 and 18), because they become aware of their physical possibilities and discover how they can make use of them by practising sport or leisure activities;

- for parents, who are encouraged to follow their children's physical development and possibly their progress in sport;

- for educationalists – who now have an educational tool that they can use as it suits them;

45

- for doctors, since it is tantamount to a medical check-up;
- for the member states, which now have a uniform test and can develop national research projects.

The nine EUROFIT tests

There are nine tests in EUROFIT, taken in the following order:

1. Flamingo balance (total body balance)

2. Plate tapping (speed of limb movement)

3. Sit and reach (flexibility)

4. Standing broad jump (explosive power)

5. Hand grip (static strength)

6. Sit ups (trunk strength)

7. Bent arm hang (functional strength)

8. Shuttle run 10 × 5 metres (running speed – agility)

9. Endurance shuttle run or bicycle ergometer test (cardio-respiratory endurance)

Notes:

(1) Survey by the University of Leuven.

(2) Paper of the Institut National de la Statistique et des Etudes Economiques (French National Institute of Statistics and Economic Studies).

(3) Union syndicale des Journalistes Sportifs de France (the trade union for French sports reporters), which controls 2,000 professional sports reporters, has only some 20 female members, although the general proportion in the profession is 60% men and 40% women.

(4) *Introduction to sport at school* (Paris, May 1976, Nice, May 1977, Luxembourg, May 1978 and final report in 1979). *Sport for school-leavers* (Stockholm, October 1978), *Sport for Children* (Tønsberg, September 1982), *Sport and physical education in primary schools* (Bilbao, May 1985), *Testing physical fitness* (Formica, Italy, May 1986).

(5) See Chapter 12 on personnel.

(6) 'Play-board', association for children's leisure-time activities in the United Kingdom; sports school for children (four age groups) in Finland; the DSB (Deutsche Sportbund) code in the Federal Republic of Germany, laying down the rules of competition for children of 12–13 years of age.

(7) Four principles: 1. Children need physical demands. 2. They need motor experiences. 3. They need challenges and appreciation of motor performances. 4. They need to play with other children.

10

Salvation for physically, mentally and socially disabled persons

Competitive sport having turned its back on anyone apparently incapable of chalking up records, *Sport for All*, more attuned to daily living and its difficulties, fills a social void because it opens physical activity to all who are victims of a handicap. An elderly person is impaired by his age, an unemployed person is socially handicapped, a migrant is disadvantaged when it comes to adjusting, prisoners have a freedom handicap, and one who is injured through sickness or accident has a physical, mental or sensorial handicap. Sport represents salvation for them all, in a variety of ways.

It is possible that even those who drew up the Charter did not immediately realise the very wide possibilities and intentions embodied in Article I: 'every individual shall have the right to participate in sport'. The Council of Europe extends that right to those who are at a physical disadvantage and who have been excluded from participation in sport, often regarded as the prerogative of healthy young men in their prime.

1.   The elderly

A very elderly person inevitably has to face a physical and mental decline, and possibly an economic and social decline as well. But the decline that is faced and mastered is not necessarily a degradation. How does the fact of having continued, resumed or taken up for the first time at a mature age[1] a physical activity possibly contribute to delaying the start of the ageing process or at least making it easier to bear? A seminar on the subject in Frankfurt in 1983 led the CDDS to publish a book entitled *Sport for Older Persons*, in 1985. It deals with a complex problem.

To begin with, there is some uncertainty about nomenclature for the over '65s, who represent 14% of the population throughout the European Community countries. Are they to be referred to as 'old', 'elderly', the 'third age', or more respectfully as 'older', as the Swiss say?

Neither is gerontological research totally conclusive, particularly on the effect of physical effort in improving functional capacities, although we do know that it helps to maintain the level of physical condition. It has been found that regular exercise reduces stress, has a reassuring effect, makes people feel more secure and confers emotional stability – all of which stave off depression and aggressivity. Group sports activity also provides occasions for new human contacts, which may well tail off when someone stops working.

Given the indifference and shortcomings of some sports federations, it was clearly necessary to set up reception structures[2] and also to find and appoint special staff[3]; the need for this has been realised in the Federal Republic of Germany[4], the United Kingdom[5] and the Netherlands[6] among others. All these countries have put considerable emphasis on campaign aspects and setting up training courses for specialist leaders.

2. The unemployed

The 1984 Malta Conference of Ministers of Sport called on the CDDS to draw up an action programme for participation in sport for socially under-privileged and marginal groups, such as the unemployed, migrants, prisoners and young offenders.

Sport can do much for the unemployed, as organisations like the Hessische Sportjugend in the Federal Republic of Germany or the Derwentside Recreation Scheme in the United Kingdom[7] have sought to show. In the first place, they have enabled the jobless to practise a sport without having to pay (or at very little expense) thanks to facilities at their disposal, and secondly they have created jobs (upkeep and building of sports facilities) or offered training (to become sports instructors or leaders).

The French National Olympic Committee (CNOSF), together with the Ministry of Labour, in 1986 adopted a similar formula for employing young persons active in sport in clubs and associations.

3. Migrants

In 1985 the Netherland government published a paper on *Sport and Minorities*, which gave a fresh boost to the policy set out in the Sports Ministers' Resolution adopted at Malta. It was swiftly followed by the Federal Republic of Germany: the Deutscher Sportbund, considering that sport facilitated social integration, launched a publicity campaign with the help of the media, calling on Turkish workers either to join German clubs, or else, should they prefer to remain faithful to their national customs and games, to set up Turkish associations which would be able to use local facilities and maintain contact with German sports authorities. This was in keeping with the two lines of action advocated at Malta: direct integration or cohabitation, in terms of sport, among different ethnic groups. It had also been urged at the two CDDS Seminars on this theme in Portugal in 1979 and 1982. (The Deutscher Sportbund and the Italian National Olympic Committee (CONI) have also concluded an agreement whereby it is easier for Italians living in the Federal Republic of Germany to take part in sport.)

It was agreed at the CDDS Seminar at the Lisbon National Institute in December 1979 that as immigrants' children were educated in the same way as nationals they should have the same opportunities without however losing their cultural identity. Sport is an ideal means of facilitating integration, lending itself to every kind of opening for human contacts – particularly between young people of different origins or races, who can join forces to defend the colours of their club, town or school. Even if they find themselves on opposing sides, sport and its rules enable them to respect each other. It is for this reason that the CDDS recommends that migrants should have as much access to sports amenities as possible.

All these provisions were confirmed and strengthened by a Seminar in Portugal in June 1982, at which it was urged that channels for communicating with migrants should be established, so that they could be better informed about the sporting possibilities available in the host countries and how to apply for the training courses open to them.

4. Prisoners

It was in Portugal again (in May 1986 at Vimeiro) that a doctrine for sport in prisons was developed where sport is an educational and recreational factor, as well as a factor making for (re-)socialisation. The starting point is invariably a humanist one: prisoners and offenders, although deprived of their freedom for a given time, are still entitled to education, culture and sport.

Living conditions in old and overcrowded prisons are so difficult that for some prisoners sport is a psychological safeguard, while for others it is just one means of maintaining their health. Some leaders' avowed intention is to use sport to prepare prisoners for eventual release, and to encourage them to go on participating in sport after they have finished serving their sentence. The organisation of sports activities and competitions may provide prisoners with opportunities for contact with the outside world, which may provide them with cause for hope. The way in which it is carried out has to be adapted to each special circumstance, but the group of experts meeting in Portugal was adamant that the Ministers responsible for Sport should fully support the setting up of sports programmes in prisons.

When the Ministers met for their 5th Conference in Dublin (1986) they considered the comments and conclusions reached by the CDDS Seminar in Portugal and suggested the introduction of an amendment into the European prison rules. It provided for the release of funds so that prisons could be given resources with which to establish adequate facilities, to buy material, and for properly training staff to carry out physical education, sport and recreational programmes. Experiments have already been attempted in numerous countries, and the Clearing House recently listed such experiments. Prison gates are opening to sport in Belgium, Switzerland, Italy, Cyprus, Turkey, Norway and the Federal Republic of Germany, the two latter countries having made special efforts to provide sport for young offenders[8].

5. Disabled persons

The Committee of Ministers, which is the supreme organ of the Council of Europe, echoing the terms of another Resolution adopted at the 5th Conference of Ministers responsible for Sport held in October 1986 in Dublin, decided two months later to adopt a 'European Charter for *Sport for All*: Disabled Persons'. What matters most for the Council of Europe, as reflected in the words of Sir Ludwig Guttmann, is that 'sport should become a driving force for the disabled to seek or restore his contact with the world around him and this his recognition as an equal and respected citizen'.

Physically and mentally disabled persons, and those with a sensorial disability, account for close on 10% of the population of all the member states[9] and total 450 million throughout the world – the equivalent of the combined population of the Soviet Union and the United States. In most member countries, there is clear evidence of a political determination to support the rehabilitation of disabled persons, and it is often a country's legislation which facilitates access for handicapped persons to public buildings, including sports stadia. Nearly all sports can be practised by persons with various types of impediments, although in most cases there have to be adaptions. Such activities are graded from top international or national competition to sport for enjoyment, or medical sport for the purpose of maintaining physical condition.

As long ago as May 1980, a Seminar organised for the CDDS by the French-speaking community of Belgium (ADEPS) urged that appropriate physical education and sports instruction should be provided in establishments for the mentally handicapped of pre-school and post-school age. Qualified physical education teachers should be recruited, while at the same time adequate equipment adapted to their needs should be made available. It was pointed out at the seminar that a mental handicap could evolve and be reduced, thanks to special measures and an environment that made for a feeling of security, and that sport could be a decisive factor here. Sport in fact fulfilled four essential purposes of vital importance for such persons – it gave them motor education, physical training, opportunities for social progress and personal and emotional development.

There was fairly widespread activity at the time to promote sports reserved for disabled persons[10]. A further Seminar held in Brussels in 1983 emphasised the need for specialist training for sports activity leaders for disabled persons.

The number of international competitions is constantly on the increase, at times without an adequate medical infrastructure. While the Council of Europe Charter encourages sports encounters between disabled persons, it is to be hoped these will be more easily accessible than has previously been the case, and better protected from certain forms of exploitation. For the mentally handicapped in particular, for whom tension is liable to be excessive, competition should be accompanied by periods of relaxation and recovery[11].

The Charter, intended for governments, is a very complete document with an explanatory memorandum; appended to it is a set of design guidelines to promote access to sports facilities by disabled persons.

Notes:

(1) 'Continued' for persons pursuing an activity after the competition stage, 're-sumed' for those who have stopped, and 'started' in the case of persons never having previously participated in sports.

(2) In 1971 Switzerland set up the 'Gymnastics Federation for older people', with 60,000 members (including 55,000 women) and then extended its activities to hiking, skiing and dance.

(3) Course in Athens: 'Training of leaders of sports activities for older persons' from 31 August to 8 September 1985.

(4) Report by Professor Heinz Meusel, describing the considerable effort made in the Federal Republic of Germany to train specialist staff and the formation of 'Sport for the elderly' clubs.

(5) National campaign in 1983, Sport and Health, organised by the nine regional Sports Councils in England, Northern Ireland, Scotland and Wales, with due regard for regional differences.

51

(6) National organisation 'A more active old age' supported by the Ministry of Welfare and Health.

(7) An indoor football tournament, held in north-eastern England in 1983, attracted 32 teams of unemployed persons.

(8) The 'Germania Adelsheim' association (remand home in Wurttemberg) organised hiking for 55 prisoners in a mountainous region and in 1984 arranged 78 sports events, more than one-half of which took place outside the prison environment.
In Northern Westphalia, 40 young inmates from five different prisons underwent 140 hours' training with the possibility of obtaining a sports instructor's diploma.

(9) It is generally recognised that the disabled 10% of the world's population can be broken down into 8% whose physical or sensory functions are reduced by 30% or more, while between 1% and 2% are mentally handicapped, most being only slightly mentally retarded. Survey by Dr Jean-Claude de Potter, Free University of Brussels, in a paper prepared in 1981 at the request of the CDDS.

(10) In 1980 the United Kingdom set up an organisation to promote sport for the disabled, and in 1984 the four Sports Councils initiated a joint campaign, with the slogan 'Sport for all disabled persons'.
   – In April 1981 a symposium was held in Heidelberg, in the Federal Republic of Germany, attended by some 100 experts.
   – Finland has put in hand a plan for the improvement of sport for the disabled.

(11) The first international competition dates back to 1948 and since the Summer Games in Rome, 1960, competitions have been repeated with each Olympiad.

Facilities

It is impossible to set in motion any movement on the scale of *Sport for All* without having the structures needed for it to start and to expand. This was something that the European *Sport for All* Charter had to cater for. Article VI recognises that the scale of participation in sport depends on the extent, variety, and accessibility of facilities. The overall planning of such facilities is to be accepted as a matter for public authorities, which must take account of local, regional and national requirements. It advocates full use of new and existing facilities.

This is the theory as laid down at the first Conference of Ministers for Sport in 1975, since when it has been up to the CDDS to put the theory into practice. After consulting sports facilities specialists and arranging seminars[1], by 1984 it was in a position to propose a body of conclusions incorporating the Council of Europe's thinking concerning sports facilities. The report of the proceedings of the Rome seminar fulfils a topical two-fold criterion: how to meet the needs caused by the development of sport and how to make due allowance for the economic crisis.

The fate of sports facilities throughout the member countries has faithfully reflected the ups and down of economic development in Western Europe. When sport first became fashionable authorities at all levels reacted in the 1970s by increasing the capacity of existing facilities and building new ones. The result was a wide variety of both designs and building methods, with different countries, regions and even local authorities drawing up their own plans. It was soon realised that the problem arose everywhere in virtually the same terms; needs of schoolchildren, organised clubs and casual users had to be reconciled. Schoolchildren, the committed sportsman and the recreational player had to cohabit and share the same municipal facilities. And with the ever-increasing importance of leisure activities, the multi-purpose aspect of facilities was coming more and more to the fore in an attempt to satisfy the requirements of both competitive and leisure sport. A further factor was the appearance of the economic recession, with a reduction in budgets and hence in projects already underway[2]. It thus became essential to make an all-out drive for value for money in building and use.

It would be hard to think of anybody more fitted to discharge this task than the CDDS, which acts as a kind of architect of European sports facilities and at the same time as its manager. Having commissioned a range of studies, the CDDS recommended different types of construction:

Low-cost facilities: costs are pruned both in capital and maintenance; in most cases these facilities are the ones selected when local authorities build them, and they often benefit from some state aid[3].

Integrated facilities: use is by all sectors of the community at all levels, and used for other purposes besides sport.

'Dual' use of facilities: which means that they are built for use by schools but open to the community in non-school hours[4].

Savings are also effected in energy use. The CDDS has made a special study of this subject, seeking relatively straightforward but effective technical and architectural solutions. One of the recommendations made is that alternative energy sources – particularly solar energy – should be utilised.

The CDDS has never lost sight of the human factor, and it does not take an eminent economist to know that the best economies depend on sound management and capacity on the part of managers. The main principle to be borne in mind here is that efforts should be concentrated on training and information for sports facilities managers and staff, but also users. There is no shortage of initiatives along these lines, encouraged by the Council of Europe[5].

Generally speaking, it has to be admitted that the work of the CDDS is effective, and has helped inspire national sports policies in a considerable number of European states. The trend is no longer to give priority to new facilities for competition, but to meet recreational needs through multi-purpose, functional facilities[6]. The publication *Planning sports facilities at a time of economic recession*[7] is a reflection of the Council of Europe's coherence: facilities as a material factor in sports provision must follow political guidelines, meet the needs of present-day society and welcome all groups, including those in deprived situations.

DOCUMENTATION ON SPORTS FACILITIES

March 1975:   Resolution of the Conference of Ministers responsible for Sport, Brussels, reiterated at the 2nd Conference, London (April 1978).

April 1979: 'Sport and local authorities' (Madrid).

November 1979: 'Integrated facilities' (London).

October 1980: 'Sport in areas with special needs' (Glasgow).

April 1981: Further resolution adopted by the Conference of Ministers for Sport (Palma de Majorca).

April 1982: 'Energy saving' (Paris).

November 1982: 'Low-cost facilities' (Marlow).

June 1983: Recommendation of the Committee of Ministers on 'Energy-saving measures in sports facilities'.

November 1984: Planning of sports facilities at a time of economic recession (Rome).

Other seminars, although not exclusively concerned with the subject, have made reference to various aspects of sports facilities, as follows: Sport for school-leavers (Stockholm, 1978); Sport for immigrants (Portugal, 1979 and 1982); The greater involvement of women (Dublin, 1980); Sport, work and well-being (Vierumaki, 1983); The challenge of increasing leisure time to sport and recreation policies (Cardiff, 1983) and *Sport for the Handicapped*, a survey by J–C de Potter, published in 1981.

Notes:

(1) See boxed section.

(2) In the United Kingdom, the number of sports centres needed in order to satisfy demand was put at 3,000, whereas the Sports Council's forecasts put building possibilities before the year 1990 at less than 1,000.

(3) In Belgium, low-cost sports halls receive grant aid from the Government; in Flanders the simple 'Sportschuur' type of hall (42 × 22m) can receive aid up to 50% from the state, provided it will be used for *Sport for All*.

(4) In the United Kingdom, the 'joint provision' or 'dual-use' principles have been adopted to denote facilities built jointly for use by the public and by schools.

(5) The Federal Republic of Germany, under the 'Aktionprogram Breitensport', advocates information for managers and users on economy factors.
   In Scotland, the Sports Council funds a computerised system for providing

information on management, and awards a prize worth £1,000 to the best-run sports centre.

In France, the authorities finance training courses for members of local authority staff managing sports facilities.

(6) France adopted this policy in 1980, whereas Italy is evolving a five-year project for 500 multi-purpose centres in under-equipped regions, subsidised by the Italian National Olympic Committee (CONI).

(7) Title of a study for the Rome Seminar, presented by Albert Remans and Marilyn Delforge, published by the Clearing House. CONI printed the full text, in two volumes, of the national reports and the proceedings of the Seminar.

Personnel

The fact that Article VIII on personnel is the last in the European *Sport for All* Charter does not mean that it is the least important. The article in question reads as follows:

> *'In any programme of sports development, the need for qualified personnel at all levels of administration and technical management, leadership and coaching shall be recognised.'*

The article says everything it has to say concisely and authoritatively, but its assertiveness gives the impression of breaking down doors in fact long ago opened by traditional sport. The problem arises in different terms, it is true, when it comes to *Sport for All*, which demands specialisation adapted to each case. This means that personnel is going to become a constant concern for the CDDS. A few years after promulgation of the Charter the 1978 Seminar in Luxembourg[1] examined the training of physical education teachers.

The basic principle posed by the CDDS is that the teacher is the most important factor in the development of sport at school. But should physical education teaching at the primary level be dispensed by specialists or by all-rounders? Although the decision does not lie with itself, the CDDS is always at liberty to put out judicious recommendations, which included the following:

- the primary school teacher of general subjects in charge of physical education teaching should receive more training for this particular purpose;

- as physical education is a subject in its own right, physical education teachers should receive the equivalent of university training ensuring that they have a high degree of scientific education[2];

- in-service training is absolutely essential and should be at the state's expense;

- consideration may be given to European co-operation, in the form of consultation services for exchange of teaching material among teachers in different countries, practical summer courses with participation of students, and periodical meetings of staff from teacher training establishments in the member states.

The 1982 Seminar in Tønsberg[3] on 'Sport for children' examined the same theme, coming to the conclusion that it was clearer than ever that physical education teachers in primary schools needed specialist training. At the same time as physical education teaching in schools was being studied, the CDDS set up its own training network, through so-called 'alternative' European courses, of training for *Sport for All* specialists.

The first idea emanated from representatives of the Flemish-speaking community of Belgium, Armand Lams and Andre Van Lierde, who presented a project to the Bureau of the Council of Europe's Committee for the Development of Sport, when it met in London in December 1977. Four years later, the Instituto Nacional Educacion Fisica (INEF), in Catalonia, invited 40 *Sport for All* educationalists to its premises at Esplugues de Llobregat (near Barcelona) in July 1981 for a practical course on sport and leisure activities for children. The course was concerned with ways of occupying school children's leisure time when they are not at school – particularly when both parents work and cannot oversee their children's free time.

Portugal took over the following year, organising a course on the possibly surprising theme of traditional sports and popular games – linked with another subject in the CDDS programme, 'Sport for immigrants'. This new course was open to 50 persons (30 Europeans and 20 Portuguese), and enabled participants to get to know traditional sports and popular games of several countries and to understand why they find favour – factors in the character of a country or region. With the aid of film and slide shows, it contributed to the exchange of experience in matters of folklore and the setting up of an Infomarket.

A third European course (Malta, 1984) was concerned with training for *Sport for All* leaders, both as a general concept and in its variety – ranging from philosophy, theory and organisation to practical work.

The year 1985 saw a still greater proliferation of initiatives with courses for leaders aimed at a specific audience, for instance: 'Sport for the mentally handicapped' (April, France); 'Sport in tourist areas' (July, Portugal) and 'Sport for older persons' (August, Greece).

All *Sport for All* leaders, even if they are qualified physical education teachers, have to cope with the wide range of *Sport for All* activities suited to the various target groups. They are responsible for the balance, physical form and safety of each practitioner, irrespective of his or her age and condition.

Doctors and medical assistants from the paramedical world also fulfil a highly important role in the oversight of physical activities for children, elderly or disabled persons: they must be able, in all circumstances and for any activity, to carry out preventive checks and provide treatment for those who fall sick or suffer an accident as a result of sport.

Despite the fact that the CDDS organises more and more training courses for staff, it has not established a general body of doctrine or a charter applicable to all the member states. The reason for this is that long ago each country set up its own physical education inspectorate and system for issuing certificates to teachers. Arrangements are already being made, however, to enable unpaid and paid *Sport for All* leaders in several countries to obtain specialist training[4]. The CDDS is watching this trend carefully with the hope that it will become widespread.

Notes:

(1) Referred to in Chapter 9, *Make way for women and children.*

(2) This is at present admitted and practised in many countries, although this was not necessarily the case earlier.

(3) Referred to in Chapter 1 under *Sport for immigrants.*

(4) France has created a state certificate for *Sport for All* physical activities, a certificate testifying to further training totalling 410 hours, spread over three years. (Decree of October 1984.)

Campaigns

Trimmy is already a legendary figure. He is the symbol and the mascot of *Sport for All* popularised in many countries through appearances on television, in newspapers, posters and shop windows, inviting the public to follow him and practise a sport. In the Federal Republic of Germany he has encouraged the whole population to discover 'Trimm dich durch Sport' (fitness through sport).

As long ago as 1970 – five years before the adoption of the Charter – one of the Trimm pioneers in the Federal Republic of Germany, Jurgen Palm, in a progress report to the Strasbourg Colloquy on *Sport for All*, said that the German Sports Federation had decided to base its campaign on the Trimm slogan[1]. It was a keyword which would enable sports organisations in Norway, Sweden, the Netherlands, Iceland and the Federal Republic of Germany, shortly followed by Denmark, to speak the same language[2]. The Germans readily admit that Trimm was spawned by Norway, where for the first time publicity was successfully directed to the actual planning of sport.

Speaking at the same colloquy, Per Hauge Moe, head of the information service of the Norwegian Confederation of Sport, indicated to his European colleagues some key formulae for the success of Trimm. Since physical sloth is all too liable to win, the object is to merge sport into our lifestyle and to do a modicum of sport every day. Trimm does not seek further to burden daily life, which has so much to contend with already, but to give man back the joy of feeling on top form.

While Norway and the Nordic countries in general can be credited with the creation of the impetus and to some extent the philosophy of physical effort within the grasp of all, Trimm in Germany has often been cited as a model for promotion campaigns in which pride of place is given to publicity, and the use of media resources. Press, radio and television help to open people's eyes, and to provide them with reasons for practising a sport[3].

All the member countries, without exception, have carried out campaigns to promote *Sport for All* since 1975, and in some cases before 1975. There is little point in recapitulating them, since their mere enumeration would fill many pages. So I shall do no more here than indicate the trends that have appeared over the last few years and comment on the action campaigns in each country.

It is clear from a recent Clearing House survey[4] that while the objective of all such campaigns is to mobilise the greatest possible number of persons in regular physical exercises, the means used vary widely in form, in financing and in commitment. The resources available to action campaigns depend on the political resolve behind them.

For example, one can distinguish between campaigns aimed at increasing the awareness of the population as a whole or of special target groups; campaigns centred round a specific sport (canoeing, jogging, walking, cycling, skiing, and also volleyball and traditional games have been promoted in this way); and lastly campaigns centred round specific themes connected with sport, such as well-being, the environment or nature conservation.

Austria gets its whole population walking and pedalling thanks to wide-scale operations reaching out to the general public, such as the 'Austrian walking shoe' (Osterreichischer Wanderschuh), 'Walking' (Langsam-Lauff-Treff), 'National Cycling Day (National Radwan-dertag), and 'Train+bicycle' (Rad am Bahnhof). As any physical effort deserves a reward, all who manage to cycle for eight hours or walk for 15 hours (male and female alike) are awarded an appropriate badge.

Belgium is a well-organised country in terms of sport, even for traditionally 'unorganised' sport. The BLOSO[5] has successfully made out a praiseworthy case for 'careful jogging' – that is to say under medical control – in Flanders. This department has another campaign, with the slogan 'Sport is great' (Sport is tof) for the period 1986–90, encouraging the promotion of sport in towns and cities[6], neighbourhoods and schools[7]. The ADEPS[8], counterpart of the BLOSO for the French community of Belgium, has developed popular walks for the general public, encouraging sedentary people to rediscover outdoor life, and has even set up a special federation for this. Another favourite activity is cross-country skiing, and every weekend in winter between 15,000 and 20,000 people hire their equipment from centres provided. The ADEPS is also concerned with adults, with its 'Point verts' for walkers and hikers, 'Stadium games' (leisure-athletics) and the 'ADEPS Triathlon' for which a certificate is awarded, on an age basis. It has set up 'School games' for the youngest, with all children in the 5th and 6th forms of primary school, taking part in various activities (walking, gymnastics, swimming, football, handball, athletics, tennis).

Sport is established on a national basis in Cyprus, albeit unostentatiously: 59% of the population take part in some form of physical activity – walking (55%), swimming (48%), football (21%), gymnastics (21%), dance (20%), jogging (14%) and tennis (7%).

Denmark aims to ensure that all sectors of the population have equal access to sports and leisure activities: 51% of the population (between the ages of 15 and 65) participate as follows: competitive sports: 18%, recreational activities: 22%, casual sport: 21%. Strenuous attempts are being made to ensure that Denmark's 450,000 registered unemployed persons can participate in sporting activities.

Spain carries out a *Sport for All* campaign thanks to the Physical Education Act of 1961 which gives sport a 22% levy on football betting takings. As long ago as April 1967 the national sports delegation, headed by Juan Antonio Samarach[9], initiated the 'We are counting on you' operation, attaching special importance to the human values inherent in sport.

Finland's campaign has the slogan 'Have a good time with sport' and is aided by the powerful Workers Sports Federation[10]. It has introduced 'Trim-Volley', a game for both sexes and with no service which all can play[11]. Activities are organised mainly locally, at the level closest to the public, and one of the prime concerns is for sensible dietary habits.

France has not ventured far from the familiar beaten track: its endeavours since 1981 have been focused on various disadvantaged groups, and initiatives such as the 500 'Sportez-vous bien' fitness trails or the discreet campaign conducted by Alain Calmat[12] promoting sport for disabled people. In October 1986 the Ministry responsible for Youth and Sports and the CNOSF (French National Olympic and Sports Committee) launched a campaign around '100,000 sports associations at your service for sport in safety'. Other initiatives include the forum train which has visited 24 regional capitals; promotion campaigns in the Paris metro and the 1987 'Games of the future', designed to make the general public more aware of physical activities.

Greece pays special attention to its 600,000 schoolchildren between the ages of 6 and 12, whose physical activities are directed and guided by 500 physical education teachers. The same applies to the 2,000 disabled children who are aided by 150 physical education teachers who have undergone specialised training for the purpose. There are another 250 leaders promoting sport for women, which in the last few years has been developed as part of a deliberate campaign.

Popular passions in Italy run highest over competitive sports and spectator sports, but in 1982 a national Sports Development Committee started to put the Council of Europe's recommendations into practice, and it has already produced results. The Central Statistical Institute has noted that in 1983 8.3 million Italians engaged in some kind of physical activity, representing 14% of the population, compared with a mere 5% in 1975 and 2.6% in 1960.

Ireland, working through its Sports Council, has been attempting to achieve the *Sport for All* objectives with all possible speed. Thanks to the organisation of Community Games, half a million children annually take part in 29 different sports disciplines. It plans to introduce Eurofit into physical education syllabuses.

The 1978 Sports Act provides Luxembourg with the framework for its policy to promote non-competitive activities. The role of the state and local authorities is defined as the provision of leadership, and suport for facilities and technical staff. The government therefore organises national days for sports disciplines stressing the re-creational aspects[13], trains specialists and encourages the provision of recreation grounds, fitness trails and cycle tracks.

Norway remains faithful to its traditional role, placing considerable emphasis on the importance of sport as conducive to health and well-being: the Norwegian Confederation of Sport has 1.4 million members out of a total population of 4 million. Five thousand of the 9,000 different clubs have a Trimm section. 42% of the over 15s regularly participate in physical activity on an individual or family basis, several times a week.

With the intention of promoting *Sport for All* in sports associations, the Netherlands have set in hand the operation 'Even I play sport' (Sport, zelfs ik doc het), more particularly geared to young people[14] and children at school, with emphasis on fair play. Special attention is paid to safety and health in and around sport.

Portugal has at all times adhered to the movement, with successive governments constant in their support for the sports policy advocated by the Council of Europe. A four-year project set up in 1983 concentrated on traditional games – a Portuguese speciality[15], holidays geared to sport, campaigns for women, children, the elderly, the disabled, immigrants and juvenile delinquents.

The Federal Republic of Germany continues to play its traditional role in the development of *Sport for All*[16]. Following its four-year plan launched in 1975, the Federal Republic first gave priority to endurance discipline (Trimm) and then to games, with the success of the 'Spielfesten'[17]. The predominant consideration since 1983 has been health, as reflected in the 'Trimming 130' form of sport and recreational activities for those between the ages of 30 and 60.

In the United Kingdom sport holds a special place in culture and education. The Sports Council, however, has set itself an ambitious target for the next ten years. It hopes, with the aid of the Milk Marketing Board and the 'What's your sport?' campaign, to step up the percentage of women taking part in indoor sports by 70% and in outdoor activities by 35%. The main thrust is towards young people in towns and cities, the unemployed and older persons. Wales and Scotland boast a large number of local projects, and have concentrated on providing a high quality of service.

In Sweden sport comes under the Swedish Sports Confederation, with its 57 member federations, each with structures in the various regions. The Confederation's slogan is 'Togetherness' and its declared ambition is to increase the number of those engaging in sports from two million to three million.

Switzerland actively furthers *Sport for All* and has created its own smaller version of Trimmy, the mascot 'Sportoli', which comes into all media and publicity campaigns. The Swiss Sports Association (ASS) has assumed responsibility for promoting and organising non-competitive activities. Its *Sport for All* committee is centring its endeavours for the period 1985–90 on the theme 'Go for fitness' (Fit-Mit), in the hope of securing the same success as the People's Olympiades (350,000 participants in 1975) and 'Gym 2000'. The Swiss Catholic Federation has entered the lists and is running a 'Sport is trendy' campaign, the most popular activities being jazz gymnastics, cross-country and long-distance skiing. There is no doubt about the success of the 'up hills, down dales', hikes lasting three weeks and covering the whole of the country by four different routes.

The personal intervention of senior political figures has been influential in Turkey, a country with a shortage of facilities. Public authorities and firms have financed the construction of multi-sports centres, particularly in Izmir and Istanbul. There are developments in the universities, five of which, out of a total of 27, have set up physical education departments. The Turkish Physical Education Directorate feels that sport should relate to customs and traditions as well: sports leaders now receive training in religious traditions.

Notes:

(1) Willy Daume, President of the German Federation of Sports at the time, and subsequently Chairman of the Federal Republic of Germany's National Olympic Committee, launched the campaign in conjunction with Mr Strobel, Minister for Youth, Family Affairs and Health on 16 March 1970.

(2) Not relevant to English-speaking readers.

(3) 650 daily papers published classified advertisements, and television put out eight shorts, free of charge.

(4) *Sports Information Bulletin* No VI, 1986, from which most of the information in this chapter is drawn.

(5) BLOSO – Flemish open air Sports Administration.

(6) A campaign for the most sports-conscious town is encouraging local authorities to have sport halls built.

(7) Special courses of action: introduction to sport, training for instructors, school sports days, study days – in particular on how to instill fair play.

(8) ADEPS – Physical Education and Sport Administration.

(9) Currently President of the International Olympic Committee.

(10) This federation, with 250,000 members and 1,568 clubs, arranges national and international competitions, the latter with labour federations in other countries.

(11) The ball is brought into play by finger contact or under-arm service.

(12) Minister of Sport (1983–86) and former European figure skating champion.

(13) 39 kilometres in canoeing-kayakking, mass walking (Man zuch zu fouss), cycling trials, sports day for the elderly.

(14) Olympic Youth Days (Jeugd Olympische Dagen).

(15) 1982 alternative course, referred to in the chapter on leadership (12).

(16) According to a study entitled *Sport for all – where from and where to*? by Peter McIntosh and Armanda Sabin, *Sport for All* was first started in the Weimar Republic as long ago as 1920.

(17) The first Games Festival was held in Essen in 1978, and four years later 300 towns and cities in the Federal Republic of Germany had adopted the same formula.

Future prospects

This summary of what the Council of Europe is doing for *Sport for All* and for sport in general has shown that over the last quarter century much has been done to promote physical and sports activities: they have become a part of culture, and a phenomenon of relevance to the whole of society, including the most disadvantaged. What has still to be done?

One reply for the immediate future is to be found in the chapter of the Third Medium-Term Plan of the Council of Europe (1987–91) dealing with Education, Culture and Sport. Further comments and pointers come from those at present in charge of the CDDS, the last two chairmen, Robert Trottein (France) and Mariano Ravazzolo (Italy) and the present head of the Sports Section of the Council of Europe, George Walker.

The relevant paragraph begins with an observation which is a tribute to the work of the CDDS and the bodies which went before:

'The growth of sport is one of the major factors in the development of western societies in past years and it has therefore occupied a growing place at political level.'

Recognising that the objectives laid down by the second plan (sports participation to rise by 10% between 1978 and 1985) had been achieved with a considerable margin, the Council of Europe goes on to ask: 'how to cope with the continuing high demand for sport, with one-half, sometimes two-thirds, of the population participating in one form or another?' It notes the positive effects of a European policy planned 'to enable citizens to take part in leisure-time sports activities, both for pleasure and as a means of . . . individual self-development', which should 'stress the positive health benefits and the possibilities for social cohesion and communication which regular sports practice offers'.

But there is a less favourable side, and reference is made to problems requiring attention, including 'those which relate to sports injuries, the potential conflict, perceived by some, between sport and the environment and the dangers related to spectators' misbehaviour'. The Plan also comments on the increasing involvement of commercial or private initiatives, and the growing financial resources made available by sponsors, entrepreneurs and the media. 'The sports organisations, with the help of governments, need to judge acceptable levels of support . . . the more general problem of the financing of sport brings into sharp focus the continuing need to defend the ethics and values of sport, bearing in mind its international character'. The personal analysis of Robert Trottein sheds light on this line of action laid down for the CDDS:

> 'The sports system evolves in a way where the economic, political, cultural, ideological factors involved and their repercussions cannot always be measured and controlled. It is not enough merely to consider the situation in terms of one group's interests, as each factor affects the other partners, who can only go along with their own logic. Because this evolution is still inadequately mastered, the moral values of sport are inevitably in a state of flux.'

Who can still defend and save them? Certainly not sport itself, which indeed had to reply on and be guided by intermediary and independent structures – such as the CDDS. Despite its own constitutional ambiguity, including as it does representatives of both public authorities and of sport, its independence lies in the fact that it neither competes with nor replaces either of them.

It can thus claim to set out a body of sports ethics, which takes into account both new partners and their own system of values. The CDDS is not an operational body: it can only inspire, prompt reflection and encourage initiatives. It must uphold the philosophical aspects of sport and be the barometer of the European sports conscience.

Dr Mariano Ravazzolo, member of the CONI[1], who took over from Robert Trottein as Chairman of the CDDS in 1987, is pursuing the objectives laid down in the Third Medium-Term Plan and the policy spelt out by the Conference of Ministers for Sport when it met in Dublin for consideration at Reykjavik in 1989.

The programme has three main thrusts:

1. Closer liaison with the other sectors of the Council of Europe

Bearing in mind the specific objectives of the Council of Europe, the cultural aspects – already a feature of the advance of *Sport for All* – should be developed with special reference to the social implications of sport. With the help of groups of specialist experts, and co-ordinated through the Committee of Experts on Sports Research and the Standing Committee on Violence at Sports Events, it should be possible to step up the study of preventive measures, the aim being to attenuate, if not to do away with, the effects of the problem of violence.

2. *Improved circulation of information among the member countries*

Close attention should be paid to the systematic and regular ex-change of information among the member states. Surveys on sub-jects being considered by the CDDS and also on themes of general interest connected with the development of *Sport for All* will be carried out by the recently established DS–SI in conjunction with the Clearing House. We will need new technologies to step up exchange of information and to set up the projected European sports data bank.

3. *Widening of contacts and fields of action*

'The Council of Europe can both contribute to the world-wide development of Sport for All, and learn from other regions. In any case, many of the problems facing sport in Europe cannot be solved by Europe alone. Contacts will therefore be developed with sports organisations, usually of an intergovernmental nature, or interna-tional non-governmental sports organisations, even outside Europe.'

George Walker, the Secretariat official responsible for the CDDS and the Conference of Ministers responsible for sport, outlines two problems, both essentially ethical, which he regards as having priority for the Council of Europe. Firstly he notes that:

'On the field of play itself, sport may of course be violent, and there the federations and umpires must punish misdeeds. The other form of violence – spectator violence – is more serious and exploits sport. Both forms of violence are absolutely contrary to the traditions, values and role of sport. Even if one can sometimes understand the temptation to violence, one has to acknowledge that sport has not always succeeded in upholding its own ethics of fair play, that is to say respect for rules, for opponents, for umpires, for results.'

This decline in values is liable to have two immediate effects: 'If sport fails to impose its own ethics and to be responsible for itself, then it leaves the field wide open to those forces waiting around sport and which are already muzzling in on the economic or political aspects. Nor will sport provide society with the examples it should, of loyalty, tolerance, respect for others, solidarity and equality of opportunity'. He is anxious, however, that proper recognition should be given to *Sport for All*, a movement which has his unflagging support and which prompts the following note of hope: 'Millions of men and women, young and old, rediscover in their everyday sports activities straightforward virtues such as friendship, help, self-discipline and the satisfaction that is derived from doing things with others. If elite sport does not always set the shining example it should, I am convinced that sport at the grass roots is morally sound, and holds out an encouraging picture not only for top-level sport but also for society in general.'

Notes:

(1) CONI – Italian National Olympic Committee.

Conclusions

In carrying out this work of investigation and compilation, in sifting the material and analysing it, I have acquired an awareness of the Council of Europe's contribution to the development of sport in general and its decisive role in the success of the *Sport for All* phenomenon. But the public is not aware of this, nor indeed are the sports practitioners who stand to gain most from it.

Will the disabled persons, young offenders, migrants and all the men, women and children who practise some form of recreational activity or physical exercise, come to realise that it is due in part to the Council of Europe? Certainly not directly, but through the ideas discussed at meetings of international experts, which then become principles and then resolutions to be finally forwarded to governments to be put into practice.

The effect of a proposal put forward by the CDDS is not immediate, because is has to be examined, studied, pondered over jointly and discussed by member countries, and, frequently, extra financial resources have to be sought. There is no quick way to surmount the slowness of administrative bodies, and the decision-takers will not be speedily convinced. By the time a proposal has become an achievement, the trace of those who put it forward has long been lost.

It is true that the press does precious little to recover their trace. The public cannot know what has happened without explanation – but the media, which revel in sports competitions and those facets of sport which highlight its spectacular nature, persistently play down any analysis of sport, its ethics and even its morals, because they fail to perceive that these are relevant to their readers or their viewers. All that concerns promoters, managers, sponsors, editors and producers of television programmes is the return for their money. This is a typical modern necessity, affecting and often debasing the destiny of sport. In some cases it needs protection, a haven where it can avoid coming to grief as it would otherwise do, pushed by that society in which it moves and has its being.

The Council of Europe is one of sports' protectors and its influence on the philosophy and functioning of sports practice in the member countries is real, albeit virtually unknown. The CDDS is a conscience for the sports movement, not only as a moral authority – in the same way as other organisations such as the International Olympic Committee or Unesco – but also in the strict sense, that of awareness of a reality and the faculty to judge it.

Index

Printed in the UK for HMSO Dd. 290318 2/90 C25 488/2 12521

73